The Politics of Home

Also by Jan Willem Duyvendak

THE POWER OF POLITICS: New Social Movements in an Old Polity, France 1965–1989 (1995)

NEW SOCIAL MOVEMENTS IN WESTERN EUROPE: A Comparative Analysis (1995) (*co-authored*)

THE GLOBAL EMERGENCE OF GAY AND LESBIAN POLITICS: National Imprints of a Worldwide Movement (1999) (*co-edited*)

LESBIAN AND GAY STUDIES: An Introductory, Interdisciplinary Approach (2000) (*co-edited*)

POLICY, PEOPLE AND THE NEW PROFESSIONAL: De-professionalisation and Re-professionalisation in Care and Welfare (2006) (*co-edited*)

CITIES IN SIGHT: Dutch Dealings with Urban Change (2009) (*co-edited*)

The Politics of Home

Belonging and Nostalgia in Western Europe and the United States

Jan Willem Duyvendak
University of Amsterdam

First published 2011 by
PALGRAVE MACMILLAN

Palgrave Macmillan in the UK is an imprint of Macmillan Publishers Limited, registered in England, company number 785998, of Houndmills, Basingstoke, Hampshire RG21 6XS.

Palgrave Macmillan in the US is a division of St Martin's Press LLC, 175 Fifth Avenue, New York, NY 10010.

Palgrave Macmillan is the global academic imprint of the above companies and has companies and representatives throughout the world.

Palgrave® and Macmillan® are registered trademarks in the United States, the United Kingdom, Europe and other countries.

ISBN: 978–0–230–29398–4 hardback
ISBN: 978–0–230–29399–1 paperback

This book is printed on paper suitable for recycling and made from fully managed and sustained forest sources. Logging, pulping and manufacturing processes are expected to conform to the environmental regulations of the country of origin.

A catalogue record for this book is available from the British Library.

Library of Congress Cataloging-in-Publication Data

Duyvendak, Jan Willem.
　　The politics of home : belonging and nostalgia in europe and the united states / Jan Willem Duyvendak.
　　　　p. cm.
　　Includes index.
　　ISBN 978–0–230–29399–1 (pbk.)
　　　　1. Nostalgia – Europe. 2. Homesickness – Europe. 3. Group identity – Europe. 4. Nostalgia – United States. 5. Homesickness – United States. 6. Group identity – United States. I. Title.
BF575.N6D89 2011
155.9—dc23
　　　　　　　　　　　　　　　　　　　　　　　　　　　　　　　　　　2011016891

Printed and bound in Great Britain by
CPI Antony Rowe, Chippenham and Eastbourne

For Menno van Leeuwen

Contents

Tables and Figures

Tables

Figures

Preface and Acknowledgments

The idea to write this book germinated during my sabbatical at the University of California, Berkeley, in the autumn of 2006. Coming from the Netherlands, a country immersed in nostalgia for the 'good old days', I was struck by a comparable nostalgia in the American public and political debate. There was, however, a big difference: in Western Europe, nostalgia focuses on the lost nation; American nostalgia focuses on lost family life.

At UC Berkeley, it was Arlie Hochschild who convinced me of the severity of the American 'crisis at home'. And though I critically engage with her work in this book, I am very grateful for the insights she has provided for me (and so many others). Also at UC Berkeley, Michael Buroway's advocacy of 'public sociology' inspired me to write a book aiming to reach a broad readership. I further wish to thank Loïc Wacquant for the invitation to come to Berkeley and the hospitality extended in sharing an office, and Irene Bloemraad for our conversations on the integration of immigrants on both sides of the Atlantic.

In the spring semesters of 2007 and 2009, I had the privilege of staying at the CUNY Graduate Center, first at the Center for Urban Research and later at the Department of Sociology. John Mollenkopf and Philip Kasinitz facilitated my sojourns and deepened my knowledge of urban sociology, that of New York City in particular. Silke Aisenbrey, Mark Blasius, Nancy Foner, Jim Jasper, Setha Low, Deborah Minkoff, Harvey Molotch, Sarah Rosenfield and Glenn Wharton have become my NYC-based intellectual companions and friends. I am grateful to them all for their important lessons regarding both academic and private life.

Back home, my colleagues at the Department of Sociology and Anthropology at the University of Amsterdam were very supportive of the project. The more I traveled, the more I realized that our intellectual community was a rarity to be cherished. I particularly wish to thank Rineke van Daalen, Annemarie Mol, Rogier van Reekum, Odile Verhaar and Loes Verplanke, who all commented on draft versions of this book. It seems a bit odd to call this book a 'mono-graph'.

Many colleagues profoundly influenced my thinking on this topic, in particular Christian Bröer, Sean Chabot, Sébastien Chauvin, Ewald Engelen, Peter Geschiere, Peter van der Graaf, Ido de Haan, Gert Hekma, Walter Nicholls, Bowen Paulle, Jan Rath, Willem Schinkel, Olga Sezneva, Evelien Tonkens, Lex Veldboer and Justus Uitermark. English not being my native language made me depend on the editorial skills of Takeo David Hymans. His excellent work almost makes him a co-author of this book. In the final stages, Robert Davidson's bibliographical support was very helpful, as was Thijs van Dooremalen's updating of the data in Chapter 3. Without my student assistants of recent years – Miriam Otto, Fleur Sleegers and Josip Kesic – it would have been virtually impossible to write this book. Fleur also contributed more directly with her fine work on the 'chronically mobile', as did Melissa Ley-Cervantes (see Chapter 2). Monique Stavenuiter was involved in the research that is now part of Chapter 3 (Duyvendak and Stavenuiter, 2010); Loes Verplanke and her students interviewed people with mental handicaps in Chapter 4 (Duyvendak and Verplanke, 2011). Peter Achterberg, Christophe Bertossi, Elmar Jansen, Dick Houtman, Menno Hurenkamp, Paul Mepschen, Trees Pels, Rally Rijkschroeff, Peter Scholten and Evelien Tonkens were my co-researchers on the themes dealt with in Chapter 5 (see Bertossi and Duyvendak, 2009; Duyvendak and Scholten, 2009; Duyvendak *et al.*, 2009; Duyvendak *et al.*, 2010; Houtman *et al.*, 2008; Houtman and Duyvendak, 2009; Jansen 2008; Mepschen *et al.*, 2010; Tonkens *et al.*, 2011).

Where did I most feel at home during these years of extensive traveling, research and writing? Alongside most others who make up the ranks of the chronically mobile, my home was indeed less fixed than in previous decades. But while my social and intellectual life stretched further afield, this did not alter my feelings of home. Home for me is not a place: home is my man.

JAN WILLEM DUYVENDAK

Introduction

We have witnessed the rise of nationalisms in many parts of Europe since 1989. The dismantling of the USSR and the Warsaw Pact gave rise to wars between states, civil wars (the one in the former Yugoslavia being the most well known) and the birth of new states. In all of these conflicts, nationalist sentiments played a pivotal role. The new millennium has also witnessed a second wave of nationalism, this time sweeping over Western Europe. Although less acknowledged, it is a remarkable development: even in those countries that have long been seen as the most progressive – such as Denmark and the Netherlands – the most heated social and political debates all revolve around questions of national identity, national values, the national canon, citizenship exams for newcomers, etc.

The framing of the nation itself as 'home' is a notable characteristic of the debates raging in Western Europe. While this is nothing new in the history of nationalism, the longing for a homogeneous national home is a novel development in those European countries that had so assiduously distanced themselves from traditions of 'Boden', 'soil' and 'Heimat' in the postwar years. Observers may be surprised by the timing of this surge in national feelings in societies that have for decades considered themselves to be 'post-national'. Western European societies have never been so diverse in terms of ethnicity, religion, and culture as they are today. But it is precisely this increased diversity that largely explains the renewed popularity of the nation-as-home ideal.

Almost all politicians in Western Europe today – from across the political spectrum – apparently believe that some people are more entitled to inhabit particular places than others. Their belief is usually based on a form of 'primordial reasoning', where places are owned by 'native' groups who enjoy specific rights (prominent among them the right to feel at home). Part of the Left's (often remarkably inconsistent) sympathy for such 'nativist' reasoning is to view the nation as 'home': a fixed place where people belong, a place which is theirs. Politicians across Western Europe champion the ideal of nation-as-home to 'support' native majorities who feel 'overwhelmed' by the arrival of 'strange' new neighbors with unknown habits speaking in foreign tongues. Many also believe that 'native' citizens will feel compensated for the loss of their communities by giving them a stronghold at the national level, where they still form the majority. If we want to understand rising nationalism in Western Europe and its accompanying debates over 'Britishness', 'Dutchness' and 'Frenchness', we need to better understand this framing of nations in terms of 'home' and the attendant nostalgia for times past.

But the often-desperate quest for the nation-as-home has unintended consequences: instead of reaffirming 'Dutchness' or 'Danishness', the culturalization of citizenship has led to endless bickering over identities, loyalties and meanings of the national 'home'. Many of those who see the reaffirmation of national identity as the solution to the current malaise dig deeper and deeper into the national past, fuelling nostalgia for a time when populations were – supposedly – still homogeneous. Nostalgic nations feel a loss of unity, of collective identity; even the most progressive among them look backwards to find a way out of their national crises.

* * *

At first sight, developments in the US may look alike. The notion of 'homeland' seemed omnipresent following 9/11. But even within post-9/11 American nationalism, notions of a national 'home' have remained much more ambivalent than in Western Europe. For historic reasons, patriotism in the US is rarely based on thick notions of place (it is hard for white Americans to pretend that their ancestors had deep roots in this land). In fact, there is a great deal of tension between the old ideals of rootlessness and restlessness ('Go West young man!') and the new notion of homeland (security).

In the US, the stronghold of 'home' remains the dwelling of the nuclear family, long seen as a haven in a turbulent world. And it is precisely the embattled family household that is central in the American crisis of 'home'. Home at the micro level is in crisis because the custodians of the traditional home – women – have left its bounds to enter the paid workforce. In fact, both American men and women now claim that they feel more at-home-at-work than at home. The American fixation on 'family values' – far from hiding the crisis of the nuclear family – is testament to it and reinforces feelings of nostalgia: while many idealize home in the past as a safe haven (Coontz, 1992), today it is an unstable and overburdened place for parents working long hours, often combining several jobs and starved for time to spend with their children. American society is deeply nostalgic for better times at home.

* * *

There is a long and rich history of research on marginal groups and their right to belong, on their home-making practices far from home. In this important stream of work, where research has been carried out on transnational bonds, diaspora, exile and the painful experience of migration, the mainstream is often conspicuously absent. At best, mainstream society is the context in which migrants arrive – the context in which they are (not so) welcomed.

This book reverses the perspective. It examines what has happened to the home feelings of the majority under the influence of the two major revolutions of our times: the gender revolution and globalization. I 'go native' by asking the majority on both sides of the Atlantic how they feel about home.

'Going native' in my own 'home country' – the Netherlands – was not necessarily easier than doing research in terra incognito. Though I have been involved in the debates on integration and multiculturalism, I have increasingly felt myself to be an outsider in my country of birth. Estrangement from my fellow countrymen made it an effort of empathy to understand their lack of home feelings and their hostile reactions to newcomers, nowadays framed as 'Muslims'. I nonetheless think that there is an urgent need to understand the lack of home feelings among the native majority in Western Europe – as there is to understand the home crisis in the US, even if that crisis seems to be of a different and less malicious nature. The gender revolution was a change from 'within' and almost all Americans seem to acknowledge that the resulting crisis at home has to be solved through common effort. This is in contrast to Western Europe, where the crisis in home feelings is blamed on changes from 'above' and pits the majority against a small minority.

The comparative perspective of this book – built upon empirical data collected on both sides of the Atlantic – should open new horizons for Western European and American debates on themes seemingly as diverse as national identity and nostalgia for times past, migration and integration, gender relations and 'caring communities'. All of these debates – at the most fundamental level – deal with the right to belong and the ability to feel at home.

* * *

'Home' and 'feeling at home' are multi-faceted and multi-scalar phenomena. Just as the nation-as-home is called upon in Western Europe to counterbalance socio-cultural changes at the neighborhood level, the fact that so many Americans feel more at-home-at-work is best seen as a compensatory strategy in the light of strained feelings at home. As Morley observes: 'If the home, the neighborhood and the nation are all potential spaces of belonging, this is no simple matter of disconnected, parallel processes. Each of these spaces conditions the others ... because these spaces are simultaneously tied together by media messages, by the workings of the real estate market, and by macro factors such as the immigration policies of the state and the impact of the global economy' (2001, p. 433). Morley is correct about the inter-relatedness of processes taking place on various scales. A fine example is given by Collins. As 'home' in the US has its deeper meaning at the level of the household, the new idea of a 'home country' had to remain close to the private notion: 'The meaningfulness of that compound "homeland" can be maintained only so long as the values of the home appear reflected in the laws of the country' (Collins, 2007, p. 11). But home feelings at one scale are not necessarily connected to the meanings attached to home at another scale. One of the aims of this book is to empirically examine how 'homes' on various scales are inter-related.

This book answers the question why 'feeling at home' has become such a dominant theme in public and political debate on both sides of the Atlantic, why the lack of 'home feelings' has come to color these days with such nostalgia. It analyzes how 'home' has been politicized, the risks of this politicization, as well as alternative home-making strategies that aim to transcend the 'logic of identities' where one group's ability to feel at home comes at the expense of other groups. In this book I therefore search for new, future-oriented home-making practices as well – practices often situated between the levels of the household and the nation – and examine policies and social movements that aim to make the 'community' the new home.

* * *

This book makes use of both quantitative and qualitative data on the multi-scalar phenomenon of feeling at home – or more often, not feeling at home – from both sides of the Atlantic. Though I address micro phenomena as well, my approach always incorporates wider structural forces that influence feelings of home; I am convinced that we cannot separate questions of how people inscribe space with meaning from social struggles involving class, race, gender and sexuality. Contrary to many psychological and culturalist studies, my analysis of home explicitly focuses on power: the *politics* of home.

These broader contextual factors invite comparison: we can only explain differences in feelings of home by taking into account variation in settings. Sentiments of nostalgia in the US and Europe may have their similarities but have different causes. At the same time, examining cross-country differences is helpful for better understanding our particular 'crises of home'. Comparing developments at the same scale (e.g., household, community and nation) in different places may also allow us to identify some hopeful trends. At the national and community levels, most Americans seem to be in less of a state of moral panic than many of their European counterparts. Though some Americans worry about losing a national sense of home (see, for example, the debates around 'homeland security' and illegal immigration), they are generally not as alarmist as Europeans. Conversely, the (Nordic) European countries seem to have found a better balance between the demands of paid work and family life, and have become a source of inspiration for American feminists.

Chapter 1 introduces the question why feeling at home has become so important to many of us: what is the meaning of 'place attachment' in a globalizing world? How does feeling at home relate to places – generic or particular, real or imaginary? How can we better understand home-making strategies? Chapter 2 examines the many aspects of 'feeling at home'. How to define this emotion? What are its constitutive elements? Chapter 3 focuses on developments in the US: its 'crisis of home' at home. Chapter 4 searches for 'best practices' where home-making has not entailed excluding others, but including those previously excluded from society. This chapter reports on new home-making practices among two formerly excluded groups: gays and the mentally handicapped. Chapter 5 deals with the 'crisis of home' on the old continent: nationalism's renaissance will be our starting point as we inquire whether greater emotional investment at the national level should indeed be understood as a reaction to migration and globalization. Chapter 6 presents the book's main conclusions and reflects on strategies to strengthen feeling at home on both sides of the Atlantic.

1
A Homesick World?

Introduction

The current era, it is often claimed, is one of big transformations. Though the processes commonly associated with 'globalization' are not new, the mobility of goods, information and people has never been so noticeable. This mobility is 'profoundly transforming our apprehension of the world: it is provoking a new experience or orientation and disorientation, new senses of placed and placeless identity' (Morley and Robins, 1995, p. 121).

For many sociologists and anthropologists alike, modernity implies mobility: 'Exile, emigration, banishment, labor migrancy, tourism, urbanization and counter-urbanization are the central motifs of modern culture, while being rootless, displaced between worlds, living between a lost past and a fluid present, are perhaps the most fitting metaphors for the journeying modern consciousness' (Rapport and Dawson, 1998, p. 23). Rapport and Dawson emphasize that 'the image of socio-cultural "places" rests on a conceptualization of time and space that, it is widely held, contemporary movement in the world now overwhelms and relativizes' (1998, p. 5). With John Berger (1984), they wonder if 'migration can more and more be portrayed as the quintessential experience of the age. ... Movement has become fundamental to modern identity, and an experience of non-place (beyond "territory" and "society") an essential component of everyday life' (Rapport and Dawson, 1998, pp. 5–6).

Many of our era's leading sociologists (Bauman, 1998a, 1998b; Beck, 2000; Calhoun, 1991; Giddens, 1991; Hannerz, 1996; Harvey,

1989; Urry, 2000), and in particular Castells (1996), have made movement ('flow') a pivotal concept in their understanding of the modern world. All claim that the increase in mobility has changed the meaning of place and space. Several positions can be identified in this debate, ranging from the total relativization of the meaning of places in our mobile era to its very opposite, that local places have grown more important due to globalization ('glocalization', Robertson, 1995). In the latter view, geographical mobility does not relativize the importance of either place or place attachment, but reinforces both.

The debate at first glance may appear of little (or merely academic) interest and unnecessarily polarized. But in what follows, I try to explain the importance of this discussion and why so many sociologists are correctly concerned (and thus fight) over the meaning of place and place attachment. Some sociologists (generally mesmerized by the changes) argue that the old categories no longer suffice: Ulrich Beck even wants to discard notions like class since they have become 'zombie categories' in the globalized world (2002). Others, like David Harvey (2000), who tend to be more negative about these changes, stick to neo-Marxist explanations to make sense of them. Here, instead of passing normative judgment, I propose that we first try to better understand what the recent changes in 'place' and 'space' mean and what they imply for our lives, for our feelings of home.

The universalists: places without particular meaning

Let's begin with what I label the *universalist* position, which relativizes the meaning of specific places. It is aptly summarized by Gustafson: 'Today, social scientists are often somewhat skeptical about the importance of place and space attachment, as people seem to be increasingly mobile, and their social relations and other everyday practices are increasingly disembedded from physical locations' (2001, p. 668). Castells, famous for his claim that we are witnessing 'the historical emergence of the space of flows, superseding the meaning of the space of places' (1989, p. 348), argues: 'The fundamental fact is that social meaning evaporates from places, and therefore from society, and becomes diluted and diffused in the reconstructed logic of a space of flows whose profile, origin, and ultimate purposes are unknown' (*ibid.*, p. 349). However vague Castells' claim may be, it clearly resonates with many people: something fundamental seems to have changed in the meaning attached to places due to the accelerated pace of our times.

Whereas all universalists ascribe a certain 'homelessness' to modern man – 'Homelessness is coming to be the destiny of the world' (Heidegger, 1977 [1947], p. 219) – they differ enormously in appraising the condition. When Edward Said (1979, p. 18) spoke of 'a generalized condition of homelessness', he had in mind the fate of those who had been forced to leave their countries of origin (migrants, asylum seekers and exiles). Peter Berger and his collaborators in *The Homeless Mind* (1973) were equally critical when they wrote of the 'spreading condition of homelessness' (*ibid.*, p. 138). Other scholars have causally linked homelessness to nostalgia: 'This homeless mind is hard to bear, and there is widespread nostalgia for a condition of being "at home" in society, with oneself and with the universe: for homes of the past that were socially homogeneous, communal, peaceful, safe and secure' (Rapport and Dawson, 1998, p. 31). Other universalists are more sanguine about certain types of homelessness. Braidotti (1994), for instance, sees postmodern nomadism as a rather positive condition (for criticism, see Pels, 1999).

Their divergent appraisals notwithstanding, all universalists agree that the consequence of *people's* increased mobility is that they can no longer develop thick attachments to places. For 'detached' people who have lost their ability to value a specific place, places eventually become interchangeable. This loss of (appreciation for) specific places is reinforced by another, related aspect of globalization: the increased mobility of marketable *goods*. 'Starbucks stores seem to be on every corner of every major city. ... The proliferation of mind-numbing sameness is an alarming trend. As the march of globalization continues, it manifests across the continent in places that look and feel alike' (Beatley, 2004, pp. 1–2). 'Today, the rapidly expanding and quickening mobility of people combines with the refusal of cultural products to "stay put" to give a profound sense of a loss of territorial roots, of an erosion of the cultural distinctiveness of places' (Gupta and Ferguson, 1992).

With many others, Timothy Beatley deplores detachment and the loss of home feelings: 'We need places that provide healthy living environments and also nourish the soul-distinctive places worthy of our loyalty and commitment, places where we feel at home, places that inspire and uplift and stimulate us and provide social and environmental sustenance' (2004, pp. 2–3). Beatley is deeply worried about the incapacity of mobile, free-floating people to connect to places that have become more and more generic, for 'meaningful lives require unique and particular places' (*ibid.*, p. 3).

Universalists agree that people's attachment to places has declined due to the increased mobility of people and goods: places have become less *attachable* (since they are less particular and more generic), while people have become less *attaching* (since they are more mobile). They disagree, however, on how to evaluate these developments: cosmopolitans view them as necessary and positive signs of (post)modernization (Braidotti, 1994). Others, like Beatley (2004), are nostalgic for the days when places were particular and 'attachable', when people were able and longing to attach, to settle down.

The particularists: places without universal meaning

What I label the *particularist* positions are in clear opposition to the universalist ones.[1] Here the places where people live continue to matter as they provide a sense of 'home' in an increasingly turbulent world. Savage and his coauthors summarize the particularist point of view as follows: 'In a mobile, global environment, location in fixed physical space may be of increasing relative significance in the generation of social distinction' (Savage *et al.*, 2005, p. 13). Perhaps paradoxically, 'an increase in movement around the world, and the freeing up of restrictive boundaries to travel, is accompanied by an increase in renascent particularisms' (Rapport and Dawson, 1998, p. 8).

Many authors explain the rediscovery of the local by referring to people's defensive reactions to globalization. According to Anthony Giddens, 'globalization and the increasing pace and impersonality of post-modern life...have led to a sense of rootlessness and meaninglessness. People lack a sense of belonging and a sense of purpose in their lives, which is leading to a search for a sense of identity and belonging in the private sphere of the home' (quoted in Clapham, 2005, p. 137). Since a detached, cosmopolitan position is 'unlivable', so the argument runs, people increasingly develop attachments to particular places.

While Savage *et al.* share the particularist view (Savage *et al.*, 2010; Savage *et al.*, 2005; Watt, 2009), they argue that the resurgence of the local should be understood as more than a defensive reaction:

> We do not see local attachments as historical residues, defensively constructed in opposition to global processes. Rather, we see elective belonging as embodying attachments that permit various kinds of global connections to be drawn. Fixed places thus play crucial roles within globalization processes. They become sites for new kinds of solidarities among people who chose to live in particular places. (Savage *et al.*, 2005, p. 53)

They further argue that increased mobility changes how people relate to places and to other people, for places and feelings of attachment to them are no longer 'given': 'Belonging is not that of an individual to a fixed community rooted in place, but rather, one in which the place becomes valuable to the individual' (*ibid.*, p. 80). 'Elective belonging involves choosing a place to live amongst your own kind, with the result that having local friends becomes an endorsement of one's place of residence' (*ibid.*, p. 85).

Like the universalists, the particularists disagree among themselves: some view the rediscovery of local places as a nostalgic reaction to defend one's own place against global forces; others see the rising importance of the local as a victory of 'choice' – a choice made possible by mobility, where new forms of 'elective belonging' facilitate 'living amongst your own kind'.[2] Part of this victory of choice is that – for some of us at least – the choice of home has become a lifestyle decision: where one would like to live in order to eat the foods one likes, go to the clubs one wants, have the shops one enjoys, etc.

Place attachments in a globalizing world

Universalists and particularists disagree over what has happened to places and place attachment under conditions of increased mobility. Have places become more or less important? Has attachment to places become more or less difficult? In Table 1.1, universalists claim

Table 1.1   Is attachment to particular places possible and/or necessary?

	Mobility seen negatively	Mobility seen positively
Universalists	1. no attachment to particular places possible; *people lost in space*	2. no attachment to particular places necessary; *the chronically mobile*
Particularists	3. strong attachment to particular places necessary; *defensive localists*	4. strong attachment to particular places possible; *elective belongers*

people have less capacity (Cell 1) and/or need (Cell 2) to relate to particular places. Particularists see people (re)valuing their attachments to particular places for defensive reasons (Cell 3) or out of choice (Cell 4).

The table reveals that scholars have different understandings of empirical reality, while diverging normative readings among both universalists and particularists show that they disagree over how place attachments matter. Only the proponents in Cell 2 are unconvinced of the importance of people to feel attached to particular places; those in the other three cells consider attachment to particular places as necessary, though perhaps difficult or impossible to attain. We also see disagreement over whether place attachment is a defensive reaction to globalization or the result of free choice, and over current and future possibilities for attachment (Cells 3 versus 4).

All except the chronically mobile understand place attachment to be attachment to *unique* places; to feel at home somewhere, 'somewhere' needs to be a specific place able to arouse feelings of belonging. In other words, they adhere to the 'one-needs-a-particular-place-to-feel-at-home' paradigm. The chronically mobile, on the other hand, don't think feeling at home is necessarily related to particular places; their relativization of the importance of particular places is based on their optimism regarding their ability to feel attached to *generic* places.

Assuming for the moment that we need particular places to feel attached, how should we increase feeling at home in our mobile world? The best a mobile person could do is to make the many places he or she comes across as particular and personal as possible. I call this the *mobile home strategy* of trying to particularize one's material world (in analogy to the real mobile home, the trailer, where one travels with as much of one's home as possible). The idea is that one can only feel at home by attaching to a specific place that is meaningful to oneself, but not to (many) others.

Imagine, however, that highly mobile people are not as desperately lost as many authors assume. Might some people not feel more at home in generic places, for instance in familiar hotel chains? Might their sense of belonging be facilitated by goods having become more mobile and generic as well? The *'generic*-places-suffice-to-feel-at-home' paradigm would posit that, for highly mobile people, the ability to feel at home is enhanced when they can stay in the same hotel chain anywhere in the world. Such people (like George Clooney in the movie *Up in the Air*) may appreciate the generic characteristics of a modern hotel: the setting, the expected behavior, the lifestyle reflected in food, drink, music, movies, etc. In contrast, they may feel excluded from specific, local places that have little or no significance to them.

Though it may sound improbable to some, I think it worthwhile to examine this possibility: that the most mobile people feel more at home in a world where goods are also mobile. Some people may actually prefer the generic to the particular.[3] The increased mobility of people would then require more generic goods to facilitate their feelings of belonging, as precisely the generic character of these goods provides these people with what is necessary to feel at home for us all: predictability, safety and familiarity (for this argument see Chapter 2).

Hotel chains can elicit feeling at home in a de-territorialized way. This implies a fundamental difference of understanding from 'one-needs-a-particular-place-to-feel-at-home', whose proponents argue that places need to be singular in their spatial manifestations. Generic places differ from particular ones in another way as well: in relation to time. For particularists, it is in and through their specific pasts that places become meaningful homes, whereas for mobile people the history of a place is irrelevant: generic places look the same anywhere, at any time, as if they have no past. When Doreen Massey writes that 'In trying to understand the identity of places we cannot – or, perhaps, should not – separate space from time, or geography from history' (Massey, 1995, p. 187), she is right for particular places. However, for the *hotel chain strategy*, history and geography matter little: generic places can be anywhere and are, in a certain sense, purposefully 'timeless'.

I will summarize all of this in another table (Table 1.2), building on Table 1.1. It starts with the similarities between the positions: all acknowledge that people as well as goods have become more mobile. The main difference between Cells 1 and 3, on the one hand, and Cells 2 and 4, on the other, is their understanding of how this increased mobility has affected our ability to develop place attachments. Those who feel lost in space because all particular places have disappeared (Cell 1) no longer have any strategies to feel at home in a mobile world. 'It is not only the displaced who experience a displacement... For even people remaining in familiar and ancestral places find the nature of their relation to place ineluctably changed, and the illusion of a natural and essential connection between the place and culture broken' (Gupta and Ferguson, 1992, p. 10). Others who share the negative evaluation of increased mobility still see opportunities to withdraw into a safe haven of particular goods and special people. These 'defensive localists' long for the good old days when goods and markets were local and people were rooted (Cell 3). Defensive localists are also pessimistic about their future chances to feel at home: they believe, alongside the protagonists of Cell 1, that mobile – and thus generic – goods undermine feelings of home for local communities.

> The chain has for years been resisted. There were a number of reasons for this resistance; among them was clearly a sense that this would be an alien importation. Many local residents conducted a vociferous and highly articulate campaign against the bringing into their 'village' of what they saw as an icon of a certain type of the brasher sort of Americanism. It just wouldn't fit; it would be completely out of place; it would spoil the character of the area. (Massey and Jess, 2003, p. 47)

On the other hand, the proponents of Cells 2 and 4 see the increased mobility of both people and goods as positive developments. The proponents of Cell 4, however, believe this mobility needs to be counterbalanced by attempts to attach to meaningful, specific places. They try to avoid generic places (like hotel chains) and search for or try to create particular ones. The best way to do this is to 'familiarize' new places by bringing aspects of one's own home – as many mobile people do on their holidays (think of the camper and the caravan). The proponents of Cell 2 have a different appreciation of generic goods and the capacity of mobile people to relate to places. Here, the claim is that it is precisely the generic, de-contextualized character of goods that allow mobile people to feel at home: the hotel chain strategy.

Table 1.2 Strategies to feel at home in a mobile world

	Mobility seen negatively	Mobility seen positively
Generic places	1. People lost in space: *No strategies available*	2. Chronically mobile: *The hotel chain strategy*
Particular places	3. Defensive localists: *My house is my home strategy*	4. Elective belongers: *The mobile home strategy*

For many people, the chronically mobile position seems like the definitive loss of the ability to feel at home. If everybody can be anywhere, one loses the ability to feel at home; one permanently feels 'out of place'. If everything can likewise be everywhere, things never really 'belong' and will be 'out of place' as well. Taken together, these trends make it more difficult to experience attachment because 'rooted' people – so proponents of Cells 1, 3 and 4 claim – can only attach to specific, historically significant places. Then, and only then, can they really feel at home.

It is here, I think, that the debate becomes truly interesting: changes in mobility have evidently had an enormous impact on place attachment, on what places mean and on perceptions of who 'belongs' where. As the following chapters will show, much is at stake. It is not just another academic debate on how to label our times; it touches upon fundamental questions of 'belonging' and 'feeling at home'. Whereas the protagonists of Cells 1 and 3 worry 'Who can feel at home today, where and with whom?', the protagonists of Cells 2 and 4 have a much more positive reading of this mobile era, including its possibilities for feeling at home and belonging in multiple places at various times (though they disagree on whether this will be in particular or generic places).

It is important to note that the proponents of all four cells in Table 1.2 agree on the importance, for all of us, of feeling at home in one way or another. It is thus hardly surprising that 'belonging' (hooks, 2009) and 'feeling at home' are burning issues in political and public debate. We urgently need to better understand these debates raging in Western Europe and, albeit in a different form, in the US as well. There are many reasons for this urgency, ranging from the importance of 'belonging' to almost all of us, to the fact that today perhaps more than before, the inclusion of some seems to go hand in hand with the exclusion of others. In this context, the term 'strategies' used in Table 1.2 should not be misunderstood. Some people obviously have more strategic options than others. These options, moreover, depend on the strategic choices made by others (multinational hotel chains, restaurants, stores, travel lines, etc.).

Sociological attachments

How, then, to approach issues of belonging? Though one may expect some guidance from sociology, the discipline itself is no neutral observer. Sociologists have historically sided with cosmopolitan ideals, while sociology's development as an academic discipline has often been intertwined with modernization's ambitions of freeing people from localism and particularism. While the founding fathers of sociology were worried by the melting of tradition, most welcomed the new freedoms of the modern world, including the freedom to migrate. No wonder, then, that in many sociological writings on globalization, 'mobility and cosmopolitanism appear to be the norm, whereas local attachment is rather regarded as a deficiency and deviation from this norm' (Gustafson, 2001, p. 668). Morley, discussing the field of Cultural Studies, writes:

> The critique of various forms of supposed essentialism has, on occasion, led to a rather uncritical celebration of all notions of mobility, fluidity and hybridity, as themselves intrinsically progressive. In that celebratory writing the focus is usually on people's ability to remake and refashion their identities in empowering ways. However…insufficient attention is often paid both to the processes through which the forms of cultural capital with which people can refashion their identities are unequally distributed,

and to the extent to which many people are still forced to live through the identities ascribed to them by others, rather than through the identities they might choose for themselves. (Morley, 2001, p. 427)

Numerous sociologists have argued that, as particular places fade away, the possibility to connect to these places will disappear as well. In their view, this is not necessarily a development to deplore.

Sociologist James Jasper, critical of the cosmopolitan a prioris of many social scientists, traces the assumptions of his colleagues to their habitus:

Academics are notoriously rootless, beginning with college and graduate school but often continuing later, as the most successful are happy to move from one university to another, every few years, in pursuit of higher salaries and prestige. As a result, perhaps, they have spun elaborate theories about the importance of meritocracy (from which they think they benefit), but few about the benefits of staying put. They would claim that their real community is that of colleagues scattered around the globe. ... Their ideal is the cosmopolitan equally at home in Chicago or Frankfurt; but is this person really at home anywhere? Ever since academics took over American intellectual life in the 1950s and 1960s, they have suppressed any voices arguing for allegiance to place. (Jasper, 2000, p. 248)

But it is not only sociologists who embrace the idea of the chronically mobile that home and home feelings can be attached to generic as well as to particular places; numerous Americans, for whom mobility has always been culturally important, also embrace this idea. To better understand the current 'crisis of home', we first examine this American debate. As we will see, there is more to American history than just idealization of the 'wanderer': fear of the unbounded, the restless and the overly mobile has a long tradition as well. 'The longing for familiarity, for a community, that is home, is a central theme in American history' (Stein, 2001, p. 215). As it turns out, there are quite a few Americans who use 'the positive language of "home truths", of the virtues of the "home-made" – and of the idea of "settling down" as itself an index of maturity. This is a terminology in which to be (too?) mobile is implicitly a moral failing' (Morley, 2001, p. 430).

The United States: restless and rootless?

Mobility and modernity are closely related. It comes as no surprise, then, that the most 'modern' of all countries sees itself as a ' "restless nation" ... The story about America is a story about movement' (Jasper, 2000, p. xii). The idea of restlessness reaches back to historian Frederick Jackson Turner, whose influential 1893 'Frontier Thesis' argued that the key to American vitality could be found in relentless movement. In his wonderful book, Jasper shows how constitutive elements of the American dream – the opportunity to move, to move up, to escape, to change identities, to be free of government, to value immigration – are all bound to the positive appraisal of mobility.

> Few Americans feel tied to their geographical location, and those who do often seem old-fashioned or misguided to the rest of us; the farmer resisting the encroachment of the suburbs, the members of inner-city gangs whose territoriality makes them loyal to their 'hood', the old lady who has lived in the same peeling house all her life. The educated, the powerful, the energetic Americans, those with a future, are ready to move in pursuit of that future. They wonder why the rooted ones don't exclaim, 'I've got to get out of here and make something of myself.' Millions of immigrants worldwide are ready to risk everything they have for a chance to come here and do just that, and millions of native-born Americans move and start over each year. This is the modern dream, a utopia in which individuals control their destinies. (Jasper, 2000, p. 242)

For many Americans, there is an intimate connection between moving and moving up. 'Americans ... try to define their identity by their lack of place: we see ourselves as people who are ready to move anywhere to take advantage of new opportunities. For us the road itself is a place, in fact our favorite place' (*ibid.*, p. 246). It is indeed true that Americans are more mobile than Europeans. Whereas Americans move on average at least every five years,

Europeans do so, at most, every ten years (and often not as far away as Americans). However, the greater *physical* mobility of Americans – which has been declining somewhat over the past decades (Fischer, 2010) – does not imply greater *social* mobility; in many (West) European countries, the opportunity to move up turns out to be at least as great as in the US (Alesina and Glaeser, 2004).

While overestimating the effects of (social) mobility does not disturb the self-understanding of the US as a society where people are permanently on the move, the value placed on restlessness seems to be changing. An example may elucidate: recent commentary on Barack Obama as the ultimate 'wanderer' reveals ambivalence towards the alleged American ideal of the rootless and restless man. On the one hand,

> There is to Mr Obama's story a Steinbeck quality, like so many migratory American tales: the mother who flickers in and out; the absent and iconic father; the grandfather, raised in the rough-neck Kansas oil town of El Dorado, who moves the family, restlessly, ceaselessly westward. The American DNA encodes wanderlust ambition, and a romance clings to Mr Obama's story. The roamer who would make himself and his land anew is a familiar archetype. (Powell, 2008, pp. 6–7)

On the other hand, 'There is, too, the sneaking suspicion that describing Mr Obama, multiracial and multiethnic, as rootless could become a surrogate for something darker. In American history, whites accused Indians of rootlessness before dispossessing them' (*ibid.*).

Obama's self-presentation during his 2008 presidential bid and early presidency actually seems to be the opposite of pride in having been on the move for much of his life. Perhaps in response to allegations of being a wanderer, and aware of his countrymen's ambivalence towards restlessness, he emphasizes that his 'roots' and 'routes' are all part and parcel of the all-embracing identity of a real American. It seems that his patriotism is at least partly a way to deal with his own pluri-identity and, more generally, with the enormous diversity within the US population. He seems to realize that feeling at home in an immigrant society is not only a challenge for new arrivals, but also for the native-born who see their world changing every day.

In my understanding, the very ideals of restlessness and root-lessness have in the long run helped Americans to feel at home in their country since these notions have become *patriotic* emblems. The 'self-made man', the American dream, the Western frontier, the melting pot and the classless society are all ideals held nation-wide. The integration of these mobile and rather *generic* ideals into a coherent national discourse provides common ground, stability and coherence to all (potential) Americans. The ideals are, moreover, infused by mobility (mostly within the US) and equal opportunity, and are future-oriented – more based on 'routes' than 'roots'. This is the chronically mobile position where people feel connected to the world thanks to generic, overarching, nonspecific places and goods. American ideals transcend particular places and groups of people and therefore potentially include them all, offering an opportunity to identify and attach.

This, however, may be changing. Critics argue that the post-9/11 discourse on the need to secure 'the homeland' implies a funda-mental change in the self-understanding of the country. 'The term homeland – with its connotations of native origins, of birthplace and birthright...– stands in stark contrast to traditional images of American nationhood as boundless and mobile' (Blunt and Dowling, 2006, p. 171). Amy Kaplan (2003), for one, sees this new notion of home as rather un-American. Has the War on Terror transformed the American understanding of itself as a restless and rootless nation? Has a thick(er) notion of home gained ground at the expense of older ideals? In Chapter 5, I will discuss the consequences of these changes in the meaning of home for newcomers as well as for old-term immigrants.

Nostalgia for the family: have the home-makers gone?

'Homeland' today seems to be conceptualized as the national exten-sion of the old ideal of the secure, private home. But this is not the only recent change in the American idea of 'home'. How stable is the private home itself? This is a serious question, not just in the light of the waves of foreclosures and the ongoing crisis in the housing mar-ket, but in light of the long-term changes in the meaning of 'home' for American men and women. The nation's celebration of itself as restless and rootless was made possible by 'traditional', deeply rooted gender roles. Men could be restless and seemingly rootless because there was a real home back home; it was the *conditio sine qua non* of the American dream.[4]

Jasper claims that women in particular have embodied resistance against the restlessness of male-dominated American society:

> Some attachment to place may be a universal need, but it seems to vary a lot by gender. Throughout our history, women have usually missed the community the most and tried to sustain it when they could. For some of them, this meant separation from restless husbands. And when they went, they tried to establish connections with friends and neighbors, tried to domesticate the land as a habitat, tried to maintain some connection to their previous lives. They have tempered some of the worst aspects of restlessness...It is women's tastes, preferences, and habits which have...the greatest potential as a balm for our motion sickness. Women's traditions appeal to a sense of place, community, and family that most Americans share but have usually repressed as an interference with their movement. It is no wonder restless men fear women. (2000, p. 237)

Though Jasper's description may be right in so far as it concerns America's past, women have also become more mobile and restless since the 1960s. I think that this change is crucial to understanding many Americans' anxieties about 'home'. Women's emancipation plays an enormous and underestimated role in the strongly felt sentiment that American society has become even more rootless and restless than before. Numerous feminist scholars have shown that the private sphere is rapidly losing its secure and protective character. The importance of paid work has drastically increased for both sexes, placing great stress on family life at home – particularly on women who still remain the primary home-makers.

In sharp contrast to all the theorizing about globalization and migration, the sociological impact of the (uneven outcomes of the) gender revolution on meanings of contemporary 'belonging' is rarely acknowledged. Chapter 3 will discuss the contributions of those rare sociologists like Arlie Hochschild who have done so in their work. Both American men and women now report feeling more at home-at-work than at home (Hochschild, 1997). In light of this, I read the recent emphasis on 'home', 'family' and 'family values' primarily as evidence of the deep crisis in American home feelings at home. Nostalgia is rife for safe, secure and stable places – places of refuge in a rough and tumble world. Nevertheless, the crisis at home is not only due to changing gender relations. Recent financial, economic and housing crises have caused great anxiety over the stability of 'home' at home, particularly in a country where private home ownership has such importance.

The search for a safe haven at home has been reinforced by developments at other – national and international – levels. On the one hand, 'homeland' today is conceptualized as the national extension of the old ideal of the secure, private home. On the other hand, themes associated with 'homeland' – security, anxiety, terror – are creeping into the private domain of 'home'. Anthropologist Setha Low has shown how the notion of 'home' plays a pivotal role in local fears (in her case, of the residents of Battery Park City, close to Ground Zero), due to its literal overlap with national 'homeland' discourse:

> Residents' fear, worry, and anxiety is constructed out of a discourse that is salient at both local and national scales with home as a key metaphor for the nation/state. ... Residents' fear of outsiders and foreigners entering their homes and neighborhoods resonates with political discussions of the penetration of the nation and homeland by illegal immigrants, foreign nationals, and potential terrorists. The threatened security of home becomes a psychological substitute for the vulnerability of the nation/state at war, compounded by the menace of unknown terrorists. Thus, the powerful icon of home symbolically transforms the insecurity felt about the nation-state, relocating it in the domestic realm. (2008, p. 242)

Western Europe: nostalgia for national homogeneity

Heated debates over 'belonging' and (not) 'feeling at home' in Western Europe partly overlap with debates in the US and partly have their own specific characteristics. In Western Europe, being restless or rootless has never had the positive connotations it enjoyed in the US, mainly because European countries – at least until very recently – did not see themselves as immigration societies. Nevertheless, mass migration to Western Europe since the 1960s has led to enormous changes in Europe's population, at such a pace that it was not paralleled by changes in these countries' self-understanding. Whereas all West European countries have de facto become multicultural societies, the very term 'multicultural' has become deeply unpopular (Duyvendak *et al.*, 2009; Entzinger and Dourleijn, 2008; Joppke, 2004). Uneasiness with the newly arrived neighbors and powerlessness in the face of rapidly changing neighborhoods has become grist for the mill of populist politicians. Even in countries such as the Netherlands, which were previously 'light' on nationalism, we now see a rather desperate search for shared national symbols, canons, icons, practices and stories. The native Dutch are literally invited by politicians to feel proud of their 'national home'.

As in the US, public discourse in Western Europe is dominated by nostalgic sentiment. The nostalgic wave in Europe, however, is discursively linked to globalization and immigration and not so much to changing gender relations. To be sure, the gender revolution has swept over Europe as well. I argue, however, that it has caused less fear over disappearing 'homes' than it has in the US. This is largely due to many West European countries having developed welfare state arrangements that mitigate the loss of stability at home. The weakness of the gender revolution as an explanation for nostalgia is particularly evident in the Netherlands, where women remain more prominent as home-makers than as paid laborers.

In Western Europe, the 'crisis of home' relates primarily to the changing composition of populations and the meanings attached to these developments by (populist) politicians. The raging debate around the integration of immigrants (see Chapter 5) is increasingly framed in terms of 'Who belongs here?', thereby polarizing natives and newcomers. Though William Walters developed his concept of 'domopolitics' for the US in the wake of the 9/11 terrorist attacks, it aptly describes recent developments in Western Europe as well:

> The home as hearth, a refuge or sanctuary in a heartless world; the home as *our* place, where we belong naturally, and where, by definition, others do not; international order as a space of homes – every people should have (at least) one; home as a place

we must protect. We may invite guests into our home, but they come at our invitation; they don't stay indefinitely. Others are, by definition, uninvited. Illegal immigrants and bogus refugees should be returned to 'their homes.' Home is a place to be secured because its contents (our property) are valuable and envied by others. Home as a safe, reassuring place, a place of intimacy, togetherness and even unity, trust and familiarity. (Walters, 2004, p. 241)

In Western Europe, the epicenter of the crisis of home is at the national level, though in a very peculiar way since the nation itself is conceptualized as one large home. Many Dutch have become 'defensive localists' in that they claim their ground, their territory, as their own. As I will show, in the Dutch debate 'home' is a multi-scalar phenomenon (Brenner, 2004; Morley, 2001) with significant links between the micro, meso and macro levels. Many of the country's politicians believe that bolstering 'Dutchness' at the national level – the 2010 coalition agreement speaks about 'making the Netherlands more Dutch' – will help the natives to feel at home in their mixed neighborhoods, to feel less displaced and nostalgic.

Until now I have used the term 'nostalgia' quite loosely to describe the prevailing mood on both sides of the Atlantic. By nostalgia I do not mean homesickness in the sense of longing for another place, but mourning over changes that have taken place *in situ*. As Rubenstein aptly explains: 'Nostalgia encompasses something more than a yearning for literal places or actual individuals. While homesickness refers to a spatial/geographical separation, nostalgia more accurately refers to a temporal one. Even if one is able to return to the literal edifice where s/he grew up, one can never truly return to the original home of childhood, since it exists mostly as a place in the imagination' (2001, p. 4). Regret over changes that have taken place, expressed as a longing for the past, relates directly to the meaning of places and those feelings attached to them: 'The identity of places is very much bound up with the *histories* which are told of them, *how* these histories are told, and which history turns out to be dominant' (Massey, 1995, p. 186).

Feeling nostalgic is often considered a characteristic of people on the move, particularly those who have been forced to move. This, of course, is often true. But those who stay put in a mobile world can feel nostalgic as well. They have to deal with both mobile goods (Starbucks and McDonald's) and mobile people, and often not out of choice. In rapidly changing neighborhoods, both newcomers and long-term residents can feel 'out of place'. In such neighborhoods, new immigrants often become *homesick* for their places of origin, while native residents become *nostalgic* for the good old days.

2
Why Feeling at Home Matters

Introduction

'In contemporary social theory, images abound of exile, diaspora, time-space compression, migrancy and "nomadology". However, the concept of home – the obverse of all this hyper-mobility – often remains un-interrogated' (Morley, 2001, pp. 427–8). Though Morley is surely right when he states that 'home' is often under-theorized (we will come across some disturbingly unreflective uses of 'home' in the coming chapters), the quote above overstates the case if we read it as a general indictment of the research on 'home'. Particularly over the past few years, many books, special issues and articles have appeared on 'home', 'feeling at home' and 'belonging' that not only provide excellent overviews of the research to date but also set the research agenda for years to come (Blunt and Dowling, 2006; Bozkurt, 2009; Després, 1991; Gieryn, 2000; Holloway, 2008; hooks, 2009; Mack, 1993; Massey and Jess, 2003; Moore, 2000; Porteous and Smith, 2001; Rybczynski, 1986; Saunders, 1989; Saunders and Williams, 1988; Somerville, 1997; Tuan, 1975, 1977, 1980).[1] There are also several journals publishing articles on themes around 'home' and 'belonging', such as the *Journal of Housing Research, Housing Studies, Home Cultures* and *Housing, Theory, and Society*.

Morley is right, however, that not all social scientists, let alone members of the public, make use of 'home' in a very reflective way. One problem with home is its very familiarity; people speak in terms of 'belonging' and 'feeling at home' all the time. For sociological understanding, this is both an advantage and a disadvantage. On the one hand, everybody can participate in the debate on 'home'; on the other, many already claim to know what 'home' is and how it feels. Curiosity becomes rare.

This familiarity does not necessarily produce articulate ideas about what 'feeling at home' is. This is due to a peculiar aspect of 'home' and 'feeling at home': while everyone initially agrees that we know what it is to feel at home, the moment we have to describe what it means to us, we begin to stutter. Feeling at home, then, is one of those emotions that eludes words. People may reveal, when urged to do so, that they feel 'at ease' when they feel at home, that they feel 'safe', 'secure' and 'comfortable', at 'one with their surroundings'. If one feels at home, one is at peace – a rather passive state where things are self-evident because they are so familiar.[2]

In other words, feeling at home is not only a familiar sentiment to us all; familiarity itself is one of its key defining aspects. Particularly environmental psychologists, who have carried out much of this research, stress the importance of 'familiarity' in their definition of home. From their *phenomenological* point of view, home is perceived as a safe and familiar space, be it a haven or shelter, where people can relax, retreat and care. Following the Indo-European notion of *kei*, meaning 'something precious' – from which the German word for home (*Heim*) is derived (Hollander, 1991; cited in Mallet, 2004, p. 65) – attachment to a home place is seen as a primordial sentiment (Fried, 2000) created by familiar daily routines and regular settings for activities and interactions. According to these environmental psychologists, 'place attachment is thus conceptualized as a positive place-bound affection by which people maintain closeness to a place' (Hidalgo and Hernandez, 2001, p. 274). Home then is an inclusive and distinctive sort of place with which people have strong social, psychological and emotional attachments (Easthope, 2004, p. 136).

Sociologist Pierre Bourdieu acknowledges the importance of familiarity in 'feeling at home' as well. Whereas the unfamiliar is 'out of place', home is the place 'to be' – a place so familiar that it feels almost like a 'natural' place. Bourdieu writes: 'The agent engaged in practice knows the world...He knows it, in a sense, too well..., takes it for granted, precisely because he is caught up in it, bound up with it; he inhabits it like a garment or a familiar habitat' (1999, pp. 142–3).

For Bourdieu, however, this 'naturalness' of feeling at home is not natural at all: it is culturally created. Bourdieu wants to understand why people experience places as natural – as 'home' – and criticizes scholars who fail to reflect on this 'naturalizing' effect of the familiar. Indeed, many environmental psychologists employ natural metaphors, in particular botanical ones: one is home where one is 'rooted'. 'Such commonplace ideas of soils, roots, and territory are built into everyday language and often also into scholarly work, but their very obviousness makes them elusive as objects of study' (Malkki, 1992, p. 26). In a wonderful article, Malkki points out that many 'spatial' metaphors carry this air of naturalness as well: 'Metaphors of kinship (motherland, fatherland, *Vaterland, patria, ...*) and of home (homeland, *Heimat, ...*) are also territorializing in this same sense; for these metaphors are thought to denote something to which one is naturally tied' (*ibid.*, pp. 27–8). Even 'culture' becomes 'natural' in this territorializing perspective since it seems to be naturally connected to a specific place: 'Terms like "native", "indigenous", and "autochthonous" have all served to root cultures in soils; and it is, of course, a well-worn observation that the term culture derives from the Latin for cultivation' (*ibid.*, p. 29).

The phenomenological perspective on home – where home represents familiarity, order, permanency, comfort and *place-bound* culture – has long been dominant. Home here is fixed and rooted, impervious to change – the last stronghold, in fact, against change. In our mobile era, this paradigm (which we have labeled 'one-needs-a-particular-place-to-feel-at-home') has not necessarily weakened. As we saw in Chapter 1, all particularists and even some universalists agree on this point. While the former claim that the significance of places today has increased, the latter argue that feeling at home has become more difficult due to the demise of 'attachable' places. This perspective, however, is not shared by those who claim that people can also feel at home in generic places. But even this last group shares the a priori assumption that feeling at home is important for everybody; they only disagree over what kind of places qualify as 'home'. 'Feeling at home' is – with great variety, so in a *non-essentialist* sense – an *essential*, even existential, feeling for all.

Let's look again at Table 1.2 from Chapter 1 (shown below as Table 2.1): all four cells share the idea that 'home' is important, even and perhaps especially in our mobile days. Protagonists of

Table 2.1 Reproduction of Table 1.2 Strategies to feel at home in a mobile world

	Mobility seen negatively	Mobility seen positively
Generic places	1. People lost in space: No strategies available	2. Chronically mobile: The hotel chain strategy
Particular places	3. Defensive localists: My house is my home strategy	4. Elective belongers: The mobile home strategy

three cells (1, 3 and 4) agree that one needs a particular place to feel at home. Cell 3 represents the 'traditional' situation: people are rooted in particular places surrounded by specific goods (*my house is home*). Many particularists, including environmental psychologists, take this as the 'natural' situation. Cell 1 is problematic from this 'rooted' perspective: people feel threatened by chain stores (mobile goods) taking over their neighborhoods. However – and this is often overlooked in the literature – mobile goods can, to a certain extent, become rooted in local communities (this is the ambition of, for instance, the Starbucks chain). Cell 4 shows another particularizing strategy: mobile people surrounding themselves with familiar, specific goods (*the mobile home strategy*). From the perspective of environmental psychologists, this is an impossible mission: how could people feel at home 'en route'? As we will see, this particularizing strategy is quite common and of great importance to those 'on the move', who want to feel at home as well.

In the following section, we first examine the position shared by the protagonists of the three cells which claim that feeling at home is dependent on particular, 'thick' places (including mobile places). But why would feeling at home depend on particular places? Consider the situation in Cell 2. Here people are mobile and surrounded by generic goods. Both particularists and some universalists would claim that this equates to 'not feeling at home'. I propose, however, a different understanding. The 'chronically mobile' have developed an effective new home-making strategy – *the hotel chain strategy* – which enables them to feel at home in generic, 'thin' places. How does it work? What does it tell us about the many ways in which people can feel at home today?

Feeling at home in particular places

For people who are *immobile*, the idea that feeling at home is connected with a particular place seems obvious (Cell 3). Here the particular place ('home') feels like 'one's family', familiarity being the
self-evident element within 'belonging'. But due to the mobility of
goods and other people, the native inhabitants realize that familiarity is no longer sufficient to make them feel at home in their particular place. On the basis of empirical research in British neighborhoods
that have undergone huge transformations, Savage *et al.* observe:
'However, ... this kind of familiarity, is often not enough to convey
a full and assertive sense of belonging. Rather, people felt "their
place" had been transformed so that they were no longer fully at
home. ... There was a general sense ... that reporting a sense of familiarity was not enough to stop you feeling an outsider' (2005, p. 48).

In a rapidly changing world, 'feeling at home' increasingly comes
to depend on the behavior of others who move into what was until
then a familiar neighborhood. In our days, (not) feeling at home is
increasingly the result of interactions with many others: it develops in a *relational* field. People can, to a certain extent, 'familiarize'
themselves with new neighbors and shops. But such 'public familiarity' (Blokland, 2003; Fischer, 1982) is not enough to truly feel at
home. When people feel marginalized or threatened, they begin
to view their *own* place in relation to other groups and *their* places,
emphasizing its exclusive identity. 'Home' thus becomes a distinctive, particular and 'thick' place. In our mobile era, a fortified idea
of home is appealing to many people (cf. Giddens, 1991). Whereas
cosmopolitans embrace 'nomadism' and consider the de-placement
of home as a positive development, many others struggle to belong
in an increasingly pluriform and mobile society. They deplore the
loss of a familiar home.

Feeling at home, then, risks becoming a *zero-sum* game: 'We can
only be insiders if others remain outsiders.' Those with sufficient
resources can guarantee their security by living with like-minded
people behind gates and walls (Low, 2004). The less privileged have
to deal with these changes *in situ* – for them, the arrival of 'strange'
shops and 'exotic' people changes the familiar, 'natural' order of
things, depriving them of the 'assumed naturalness of their taken
for granted identities' (Morley, 2001, p. 439). Defensively, they seek

to re-establish the broken link between 'culture' and 'place': 'Their "homely racism" (should be understood) as a fearful response to the destabilization, through new patterns of migration, of the privileged link between habit and habitat' (*ibid.*). What is felt as home, then, develops out of a dialectic between what belongs to the place and what does not; what is mentally near and what is far; what feels like 'inside' and what does not; who are considered 'we' and who are labeled 'others'.

Especially Chapter 5, dealing with Western Europe, will address how immobile people can (not) feel at home in a mobile world. As we will see, it turns out to be quite difficult, often leading to *nostalgia* for the good old days. Many policy-makers are aware of the 'hunkering down' effect that increased heterogeneity can produce (Putnam, 2007). They therefore encourage long-term inhabitants and immigrants to get to know one another and practice what Kwame Appiah has called 'rooted cosmopolitanism': 'Attached to a home of his or her own, with its own cultural particularities, but taking pleasure from the presence of other, different places that are home to other, different people' (Appiah, 1998, p. 91). Appiah argues that while being rooted is important for everybody, it need not entail a negative view of other(s') places. As we will see, this is more easily said than done. Is there space (also literally) for a *positive sum* perspective on feeling at home for immobile people in a mobile world – for them to feel at home and enjoy the ability of 'others' to feel at home as well?

Many mobile people eventually settle down and create particular places; in some contexts and depending on their reasons for moving, newcomers may even try to assimilate. Many immigrants, however, do not immediately relate to their new surroundings. They are not acquainted with the particularities of the places they have come to live in, and are not necessarily interested in them for they do not help them feel at home. When they establish homes away from home, immigrants often recreate places that look and smell, at least to a certain extent, like the places they left behind. One might say that while their native neighbors often become nostalgic for *times* when they were among their 'own', immigrants often become homesick for more familiar *places*. Immigrants, however, bring goods from their country of origin not only for nostalgic reasons; these goods can foster home-making and feeling at home in new places as well. As discussed in Chapter 1, I label this the *mobile home strategy*. It is not only used by migrants, but also by people on the move within their own countries for work or pleasure (Andrews, 2005), as in the case of the caravan and camper.

Alongside poorer migrants who have always moved and still move from one country to another, we see today a new category of 'chronically mobile persons': CEOs, workers in the transport sector, academics, people working for international NGOs and many others. Quite a few recent studies have addressed their sense of belonging and their home-making strategies (Nowicka, 2007; Tandogan and Incirlioglu, 2004). Many of these studies have found that these people can enjoy their mobility because 'one dwells not only in a place but also in travel. Thus, home should be seen as something that individuals can take along as they move through time and space... For a world of travelers, home comes to be found in a routine set of practices, in a repetition of habitual social interactions' (Nowicka, 2007, p. 72). They employ 'domesticating' strategies to feel at home in 'strange' places: they enjoy the generic places they come across (such as hotel rooms) by acting out certain habits and connecting to people like themselves (Ley-Cervantes, 2008; Sleegers, 2008). 'The very presence of familiar features from the home world of newspapers, TV programs and food serve to provide the cultural context of action and repeat the everyday' (Andrews, 2005, p. 263).

Magdalena Nowicka's article 'Mobile locations' is a wonderful example of scholarship that 'de-roots' the notion of home. She convincingly argues against the 'roots' view where the place to feel at home is a *fixed* place:

> Home [was] regarded as a stable, unmoving centre from which the world around can be perceived, conceived and experienced, and thanks to which ethnic and national identities can develop... It is considered to be a fixed environment: being at home means stationary, centered, bounded, fitted, engaged and grounded... Social science would thus choose a spatially fixed home and investigate how its particularity and atmosphere is created. (Nowicka, 2007, p. 72)

The *roots* paradigm (Malkki, 1992) thus needs to be supplemented with a *routes* paradigm to comprehend the experience of numerous people the world over. For mobile people, new places may feel like home – or become home – meaning that feelings of home can be attached to several places, even simultaneously (Anderson, 1991 [1983]; Gustafson, 2001; Hannerz, 1996). 'Rather than view home as rooted, located, and bounded, and often closely tied to a remembered or imagined homeland, an emphasis on "routes" invokes more mobile, and often de-territorialized, geographies of home that reflect transnational connections and networks' (Blunt and Dowling, 2006, p. 199).

Nowicka's perspective on home as part of 'globally stretching networks' (2007, p. 83) builds on Massey's notion of place 'as formed out of numerous social relationships stretched over space' (Massey, 2003, p. 69). For Nowicka, this implies that homes for the extremely mobile are more socially than territorially defined: they are more about the people one interacts with, the familiar faces, etc. In this way, her work transcends the 'one-needs-a-particular-place-to-feel-at-home' paradigm. Nowicka says little, however, about the nature of the people and objects that make the highly mobile feel at home; she only notes that 'home is being established around particular relationships to people and objects' (2007, p. 81). I propose that for the very mobile, this 'particular relationship' is often determined by the *generic* quality of places, and that home can therefore be even more radically de-territorialized than Nowicka suggests.[3] Let's now consider the issue of generic places before turning to non-territorialized homes and ways of feeling at home.

Feeling at home in generic places

In the literature, it is often suggested that mobile people – like their non-mobile brethren – look for particular places to connect with. The findings of my research team (see also Ley-Cervantes, 2008; Sleegers, 2008), however, point in a different direction: for the very mobile, particular places matter little. They don't consider them very 'attachable' and prefer more generic places. While some researchers consider the increasing mobility of people and goods to be undermining our ability to feel at home, the opposite seems to be true for the most mobile: it is precisely the spread of generic goods that enables them to feel at home in various places.

All people – the very mobile included – still can and want to 'attach', even if the very mobile are often painted as 'rootless' individuals. To feel at home they need, like everyone else, 'attachable' goods. For the highly mobile, these goods are necessarily of a generic nature as local goods will have little significance for them (local communities may even be experienced as intimidating). While worldwide hotel chains may be considered 'alien' by many locals, they resemble 'home' for the mobile rich. In fact it would be a risky strategy for these hotel chains to become 'rooted': if they were to reach out to the community – to 'go native' – they would lose their generic characteristics and ability to provide a home-like context for the most mobile.

The generic nature of these places around the globe provides a familiar context for a specific, highly mobile group of people. They can feel at home, not because of the particularity of the place – its history, rootedness or local meaning – but because of its general, a-historical and, indeed, 'light' nature. Whereas most scholars claim that people need 'thick', particular places to feel at home, for some groups the 'thin' character of generic places aids home-making. Their 'homes' are interchangeable places, almost 'non-places'; their hotels, airports and business centers are 'footloose'. The very fact that these spaces are 'thin' on particular traits makes it easier for the chronically mobile to 'lightly' particularize them: 'I bring books and magazines as well as candles to have a familiar scent from home' (Sleegers, 2008, p. 71).

While the most mobile and the most immobile differ on the importance they attach to particular places, what makes them feel at home is the same. For both, *familiarity* is a necessary, though not a sufficient, condition to feel at home. In the privileged case of the rich and highly mobile, familiarity is guaranteed in the 'non-places' we have described. But there is more to these places than just familiarity. These 'footloose' spots are also predictable, secure, and often segregated.

All these aspects reinforce feeling at home, of being among one's own kind (in this case often among businessmen, journalists, colleagues from academia, etc.): 'Besides my friends, the people I get attached to are global travelers, people who have traveled and lived in other countries and have experienced the same lifestyles – they are the ones whom I can more readily relate to' (*ibid.*, p. 65). Highly mobile people feel at home with others like themselves in recognizable spaces of a generic character.

While immobile people are basically seeking the same things (pre-dictability, safety and protected places), they often feel they must defend the particularity of their own places against the threat posed by mobile people and goods (de Gruijter *et al.*, 2010). 'Foreigners ruin the neighborhood', said an older woman we interviewed in The Hague. Especially elderly long-term residents tend to view new arrivals as threats. The latter are held responsible for reduced social contact in the neighborhood, the disappearance of local shops, an increased sense of insecurity and even the district's 'degradation'. The presence of 'criminal immigrants' undermines the ability to feel at home in the neighborhood. Such feelings, however, often go beyond the facts. The woman in question could not mention any specific instances of 'aggressiveness' on the streets: 'Actually, everything still went well, but you sometimes hear and see things' (Tonkens *et al.*, forthcoming).

Whereas the immobile withdraw to feel at home (Cell 3), the mobile rich have more options (Cell 2, though the number of places with generic characteristics is still limited). Crucially, the rich-and-mobile can financially secure their feeling at home; they also have the option to move on. This exit option is in itself a form of security, which the immobile lack.

All this shows that there are important differences between the places where more and less mobile people feel at home: whereas the former need particular, historic and context-specific places, the latter long for generic places that could be anywhere. This is not to say that the latter feel at home everywhere – that 'the world is their home', as the cosmopolitans would have it. The very mobile feel at home in generic places that are still quite rare in the world. Generic places, moreover, do not mean neutral places: the hotels, airports and car rental centers cater to specific groups of (mostly) privileged Western men who may well keep 'particular' goods and people at arms length as they threaten their sense of comfort. In this sense, I tend to disagree with authors who claim that the very mobile are able to integrate the 'alien' into their feelings of home – that they can accept home experienced as 'strange'. But such is the claim by Ahmed (1999), who rejects the idea that home and away are oppos-itional concepts and experiences. For her, 'home encompasses both movement and strangers. Home can be experienced as strange and/or familiar' (paraphrased in Mallet, 2004, p. 78).

The differences between the more and less mobile often run parallel with class; their divergent ways of feeling at home often have class-specific consequences. First, the spread of the generic places of the rich-and-mobile may threaten the poor, who may be displaced to create space for 'generic development'. Second, it is not only generic goods for the rich-and-mobile (like hotel chains) that are spreading around the world. Starbucks and McDonald's do so as well, catering to many less mobile inhabitants. Third, clashes between the more and less mobile are not always clashes between rich and poor. As we all know, poor people are themselves often highly mobile, as victims of wars or pushed by poverty and lack of opportunities in their own villages, cities and countries. For these people, migration is often a disturbing experience, particularly for their feelings of home. In cities and neighborhoods in their countries of arrival, they can unintentionally upset the jealously guarded places of the (often relatively disadvantaged) native population. Mobility in the form of migration of the poor tends to disproportionately affect disadvantaged groups in countries of arrival. Next to inter-class relations, intra-class relations become tense as well.

The coming chapters will deal with numerous aspects of mobility. We will pay attention to relations between groups, since one group's feeling at home often depends on that of others. The chronically mobile – although small in number – are interesting as they point to new ways of feeling at home that have largely been neglected in the literature thus far. At the same time, we will retain our focus on those who are considered the 'losers' of globalization since their home feelings are the most seriously threatened.

Beyond the particular and the generic: the symbolic

In order to map the possible aspects of 'feeling at home', we have to deal with yet another element. Both particular and generic perspectives still relate feeling at home to *concrete* dwellings and places. Even when home is conceptualized as being on the move, most scholars still link feeling at home to a *material* place. But 'home', I argue, does not need to be a material, geographical place. Feelings of home can also be attached to a virtual space (Mallet, 2004): since the ICT revolution, more and more people feel at home in the virtual worlds of their laptops. Others locate 'home' within sacred structures

(Manzo, 2003): many Muslims, for instance, feel most at home in the Umma. In the coming chapters we will come across several examples of such non-territorialized homes. We thus need to go beyond the four positions in Table 2.1, all based on the idea that we are dealing with a feeling that, in one way or another, is directly related to a physical place.

We should, however, be wary of stretching the argument too far. The fact that symbolic, non-material homes exist is no reason to claim that home is only or always imagined. The immaterial home will often be linked to concrete manifestations of 'home' in the past or present, or be a projection of a concrete home in the future.[4] We rarely find examples of home that are purely symbolic: 'Home [as] a spatial imaginary: a set of intersecting and variable ideas and feelings, ... are related to context, and ... construct places, extend across spaces and scales, and connect places' (Blunt and Dowling, 2006, p. 2).

Perhaps the most relevant way to think about the symbolic character of home is not as detached from the material world but as *signifier* of this world, since the material world has no meaning in itself. As Easthope puts it: 'While homes may be located, it is not the location that is "home"' (2004, p. 136). He correctly distinguishes between 'home' and 'house', showing that a house only becomes a home as meanings and feelings – in other words, a certain symbolic value – become attached to it. This implies that the material world in itself has no real 'home value'; for this it needs meanings and feelings to be attached. 'Home is grounded less in a place and more in the activity that occurs in the place' (Jackson, 1995, p. 148). 'Home', then, is more the result of home-making than the effect of the place itself. Places do not intrinsically have home-like characteristics (safe, secure, welcoming, etc.); we develop these feelings for places over time. This is evident when we look at 'familiarity' – so fundamental to feeling at home. Familiarity takes time.

The constructionist critique that 'objective' places do not in and of themselves evoke self-evident, 'natural' feelings of belonging questions a priori distinctions between more or less home-like places. Much of the literature, however, seems to have set ideas about where home belongs; it does not expect people to feel at home outside their houses, in hotels, at their workplaces, or in anonymous environments. Instead of starting from a normative idea of what 'home' should be, I propose to listen to what people say regarding where and when they feel at home, and what feeling at home means to them.

Meanings of home

For now, the only thing we know for sure is that 'home' matters to all. But what is it to 'feel at home'? In my research, I came across many meanings of home for various people. This multiplicity is itself meaningful: to 'feel at home' is not a singular feeling but a plural and layered sentiment that travels from the individual household via the neighborhood to the nation, and from the house to the workplace. Nevertheless, we can draw some tentative conclusions regarding the possible meanings of home. First, 'familiarity' is a necessary but often insufficient condition for feeling at home. Other factors that may play a role resemble those aspects Rybczynski lists in *Home: A Short History of an Idea* (1986) that make a house feel like home: intimacy and privacy, domesticity, commodity and delight, ease, light and air, efficiency, style and substance, austerity and comfort and well-being. If we leave out the material, house-bound elements, we have a list that resembles those of many other authors as well. In their intriguing *Domicide: The Global Destruction of Home* (2001), Porteous and Smith discuss the classifications of scholars who have been struggling with the many possible meanings of home. Summarizing their findings as well as the meanings I came across in numerous articles and books, I come to the following basic classification of the 'elements of home':

I. **Familiarity**
   'Knowing the place'
II. **Haven: secure, safe, comfortable, private and exclusive**
   Physical/material safety; mentally safe/predictable
   Place for retreat, relaxation, intimacy and domesticity
III. **Heaven: public identity and exclusivity**
   A public place where one can collectively be, express and realize oneself; where one feels publicly free and independent. Home here embodies shared histories; a material and/or symbolic place with one's own people and activities

This, to be sure, is a rudimentary typology (Setha Low [2004] speaks along similar lines of a 'fort' and a 'castle'), but it will prove helpful in my quest to better understand what people mean when they say they do (not) feel at home. The first aspect – familiarity – has already been discussed at length: it is the precondition for the other two. 'Haven' covers aspects of home that pertain to feelings of safety, security and privacy, which most often relate to the micro level of the house. Those aspects of home that come under the heading of 'heaven' (Porteous and Smith, 2001, p. 44) are more outward-oriented and/or symbolic: they help individuals to 'be', develop and express themselves collectively, and to connect with others, often through the creation of intentional communities. In terms of Table 2.1, the haven concept of home always relates to particular places: either in the form of defensive localism (Cell 3) or elective belonging (Cell 4). Home-as-heaven can be a particular place (a neighborhood, a city or even a nation) but can also develop in rather generic places (see the example of gay neighborhoods discussed in Chapter 4).

But whether experienced as haven or heaven, feeling at home is a highly selective emotion: we don't feel at home everywhere, or with everybody. Feeling at home seems to entail including some and excluding many.

The emotion of feeling at home

Social scientists who write about emotions largely overlook 'feeling at home' and 'belonging'. The reverse is true as well: those who write about 'home' usually focus on the physical 'home' rather than on the 'feeling', and rarely consider 'feeling at home' from the perspective of theories of emotion. How can this mutual neglect be explained?

Let's begin with those who study emotions. First, the scant attention paid to 'feeling at home' – by social psychologists and sociologists alike – may be related to the idea that they deal with 'emotions' and not 'feelings'. But if we look at the definitional confusion that characterizes the literature on 'feelings', 'emotions' and 'affects', this argument is difficult to sustain. Some authors assert that the main difference between *emotions* and *feelings* lies in the subjective and conscious character of feelings versus the physical, unreflective character of emotions. Others assert that the difference between *affects* and *emotions* is that affects are physical while emotions are conscious phenomena. Turner and Stets write that 'most theorists and researchers in sociology would define feelings as emotional states about which a person is consciously aware' (Turner and Stets, 2005, p. 286), implying that emotions as such lie outside conscious experience. This resonates with Damasio's differentiation of 'emotions' and 'feelings', where emotions are 'objectively observable organic processes whilst "feelings" are the subjective experience of emotions' (in Greco and Stenner, 2008, p. 12; see also Damasio, 1999). However, Greco and Stenner in their recent book argue that 'affects' constitute a new and necessary field for sociological research; due to the 'textual turn' in the social sciences, emotions have become 'discursive, dialogical phenomena' (Greco and Stenner, 2008, p. 9). They argue that the 'affective turn' is informed by the difference between affects and emotions, where 'emotion is a more superficial and conscious affair, whilst affect refers to deep and often unconscious organismic processes' (*ibid.*, p. 10). We have thus come full circle: here 'emotions' mirror 'feelings' as defined by Turner and Stets (2005). Whatever the 'correct' definition, there is no longer an excuse for social psychologists and sociologists dealing with emotions/feelings/affects to overlook the importance of 'belonging' and 'feeling at home'.

A second reason why specialists on emotions (and feelings and affects) don't deal with 'feeling at home' might be the emotion's grab-bag character. We have seen that feeling at home is a multilayered, multi-scalar phenomenon. Moreover, familiarity in itself is insufficient to feel at home. To really feel at home, many other emotions – which differ for individuals, situations and time periods – enter the fray: the *haven* emotions that go with a safe, comfortable and predictable place, the *heaven* emotions where one is able to be 'oneself' in public and feel connected. Has perhaps the grab-bag quality of 'feeling at home' deterred sociologists and social psychologists from seriously investigating it?

Another possible explanation is that 'feeling at home' does not lend itself to easy investigation. As already mentioned, for many people the feeling itself is difficult to describe, in contrast to the many stories that they can tell about how they got to know a place:

> Sense of place is rarely acquired in passing. To know a place well requires long residence and deep involvement. It is possible to appreciate the visual qualities of a place with one short visit, but not how it smells on a frosty morning, how city sounds reverberate

across narrow streets to expire over the broad square, or how the pavement burns through gym shoe soles and melts bicycle tires in August. (Tuan, 1975, p. 164; see also Tuan, 1980)

Moreover, most people know very well when and where they do *not* feel at home. Then it becomes a powerful emotion – people want to feel at home somewhere, and will do anything to keep or regain that feeling. It then also becomes a very 'telling' emotion: people can tell long stories about when and where and why they do not feel at home. But though one takes action to feel at home (again), once achieved the feeling becomes passive and inactive. This may offer a fourth explanation for social science's scant interest in 'feeling at home': most of the time, it does not lead to vigorous action and thus sits uneasily with the claim of the famous psychologist of emotions Nico Frijda that 'emotions exist for the sake of action' (2004, p. 170).

Though this remains a plausible reason to exclude 'feeling at home' from textbooks on emotions and feelings, the absence is strange. Not feeling at home is a powerful emotion – perhaps not a primary one, but, as both American and West European politics have revealed in recent years, connected to primordial sentiments of who 'belongs' where: in one's house, neighborhood, city or country. 'Home' and 'feeling at home' are central within the emotionalization of politics and the culturalization of citizenship (hooks, 2009; Isin *et al.*, 2008; Schinkel, 2008) and now stand at the heart of public and political debate. This last development should be sufficient reason for social scientists to take 'feeling at home' seriously.

Why, on the other hand, have authors who write about 'home' paid relatively little attention to its emotional side? This is not easy to answer either. One possible reason is that the sociology of emotions has until very recently been an underdeveloped area within the discipline. It had little to offer to the sociologists of 'home' (van der Graaf, 2009).

Sociologists wishing to explore 'feeling at home' thus needed mainstream support to buttress the legitimacy of their research. Were not 'home' and 'feeling at home' too pedestrian, too vague for serious investigation? If these subjects were already being discussed on the street, in the cafes, at dinner tables, in the newspapers and in parliament, what more could social scientists hope to contribute?

In response to the reproach that they were investigating an all-too-familiar subject, social scientists sought a sturdier foundation for their research: attention now turned, not to the 'soft' world of emotions, but to the 'harder' context of place. But while concepts such as 'place attachment' were well received, the *emotion* of 'feeling at home' attracted less interest than the *object* of the feeling, the place qua place. This neglect of the emotion-as-emotion appeared to suggest that 'feeling at home' meant and was experienced by everybody as the same thing. Moreover, the research focused on the material objects through which people felt at home in given places, effectively sidelining those symbolic and imaginary aspects that also inform the feeling. Transnational 'belonging' in the Umma, for example, appeared exotic, outside the investigative scope of sociologists in general as well as of scholars researching 'feeling at home'.

There were, of course, inspiring exceptions. Arlie Hochschild, one of the pioneers in the sociology of emotions, sought to earn for emotions a legitimate place within sociology; emotions, after all, were social phenomena through and through. But while 'home' has a prominent place in Hochschild's work, it seems that even she did not really think it through as an emotion. This we will see in the coming chapter.

3

Losing Home at Home: When Men and Women Feel More at Home at Work

Introduction

Home – here understood as the place where people live and sleep – has always been highly gendered. Women have historically been associated with 'home' and remain until our day the primary 'home-makers' (Fuwa, 2004; Hareven, 1983; Jasper, 2000, p. 235; Mallet, 2004; Perrot, 1990; Simmel, 1984). The growing incidence of women working outside the home in many Western countries has thus altered the situation at home. Particularly in the US, numerous authors (Gerson, 2004a, 2004b; Gerson and Jacobs, 2004; Gornick and Meyers, 2003; Jacobs and Gerson, 2004b; Schor, 1991) describe the consequences of the gender revolution in highly alarmist tones: Americans suffer from a 'time squeeze', feel overworked and have little time for home.

This marginalization of family life in the US is the result of many factors, such as the lack of welfare state provisions and the growing importance of paid work for all Americans – for both men and women. This has been accompanied by the blurring of boundaries between 'home' and 'work' (Epstein and Kalleberg, 2004): home has become work (Conley, 2009) and work has become home (Hochschild, 1997).

The promise of the service economy to create more leisure time (Epstein and Kalleberg, 2004; Jacobs and Gerson, 2004b; Robinson and Goodbey, 1997) has simply not materialized for most Americans, neither for those at the top of the job ladder nor for those at the bottom. As we will see, many Western heterosexual couples – and not only Americans – spend more time at work today, largely due to women's greater participation in the labor market.

Home as hell; home as haven/heaven?

In most Western countries, the women's liberation movement of the 1960s and 1970s aimed to decouple women and home: women, its proponents argued, should be welcomed onto the labor market while men should take up their fair share of housework and child-rearing (Friedan, 1963; Hochschild, 1989; Pateman, 1989). For many women, paid work was indeed an important step into the outside world.

'Home' had negative connotations for the early women's movement. The American feminist Betty Friedan famously described the home as an oppressive place for women, a place that confines them to the domestic sphere. Home was a trap (Weintraub and Kumar, 1997) and sometimes even hell: 'As a symbolic representation, home serves to remove women from the "real" world of politics and business.... As lived experience, home can be similarly oppressive.... For many women, home is a space of violence, alienation and emotional turmoil' (Blunt and Dowling, 2006, p. 15).

Though home in its gendered version has been heavily criticized, 'home' has survived as an ideal. The new dreams were based on homes with men and women sharing equally in housekeeping, child-rearing and paid labor. Home no longer needed to be a 'haven in a heartless world'. The new home beyond stereotypical gender roles promised 'heaven' – a place for self-realization and self-expression open to the world, embedded in shared services provided by the neighborhood community (Hayden, 2002).

But this dream never materialized. While women entered the labor market in impressive numbers, men didn't take over household tasks to a comparable degree. Households in many Western countries were thus confronted with a crisis at home – one which has been particularly acute in countries such as the US where women began working full time without the benefits of a welfare state.

Prominent feminists of the 1960s and 1970s like Arlie Hochschild were shocked by this unintended consequence of the gender revolution: their idea had been to transform home, not to abolish it.

In their view, the *demise* of home was now the main problem –
for women and men alike. In her work through to *Global Woman*
(together with Ehrenreich, 2003),[1] Hochschild largely holds men
responsible for the crisis at home. She addresses the necessity of
men to contribute more to care tasks in order to unburden women
of the *second shift* of housekeeping, to create more harmonious heterosexual relationships and to let Third World women care for their
own children instead of working as nannies in the US. Nevertheless,
the emphasis of Hochschild's work has clearly changed. Whereas
her famous *The Second Shift* (1989) focused on the fairer distribution of housework between men and women in joint households,
The Time Bind (1997) focused on the distorted relationship between
'work' and 'home'. Rather than emphasizing the unfair *differences* in
men and women's contributions, she now points to the *similarities*
in their hard-working lives. Whereas capitalism in the 1970s was
blamed for trapping women in the home – and profiting from their
unpaid 'reproductive' housework – capitalism today is blamed for
trapping women (and men) at work and not providing enough time
to be at home.

Below I reconstruct what the gender revolution has meant for
American men and women and their 'crisis at home' and compare
the situation in the US to that of Western Europe, where households
have been less affected by market forces. This reconstruction largely
draws on the work of Arlie Hochschild, who has written on home
and work for the better part of three decades. In the second part of
the chapter, I analyze underlying notions of 'home' in the work of
the main protagonists in the debate on the future of the work–care
balance. What is their understanding of home? Where do they situ-
ate 'home'? And last but not least: is the market the main threat to
the real 'home' or the new place for people to feel at home?

The marginalization of home in the US

A new political fervor has emerged among American women who
toil under the double burden of housekeeping and a full-time job.
Groups such as MomsRising in the *Motherhood Manifesto* stress that
women today are much too busy. They point out that the US and
Australia are the only industrialized countries with no paid mater-
nity leave, poor childcare facilities and few days of paid vacation.

The situation is dire enough to encourage (higher class) women to stay at home (Yang and Rodriguez, 2009).

The sense is that Americans are overworked and time-squeezed. 'Basic social changes are placing increasing pressures on workers and their families. ... Family time is squeezed because more household members are employed. The rise of dual-earning couples has contributed to a large increase in the combined working time of married couples' (Jacobs and Gerson, 2004b, pp. 41–2). The same criticism is heard repeatedly within public, political and academic debate – at issue is 'the legitimacy of time demands at work, the sacrifice of other values to the ever-faster production of goods and services, and the resulting burden placed on the family and the health of citizens' (Epstein and Kalleberg, 2004, p. 2).

This new situation causes real anxiety among Americans, and not just among those with the most precarious jobs: 'The increasingly important role that women play in the economic life of a family forms the bedrock of the real story of middle-class anxiety. That's because household labor – most notably child care – has not gotten any easier in the meantime. Blending work and home responsibilities is no easy feat, especially in a 24/7 service economy that allows many of us to work from home at all hours' (Conley, 2009, p. 13).

Hochschild emphasizes that women – due to their increased participation in the labor market and the 'squeeze' at home – are becoming similar to men in the values they ascribe to home and work. Whereas men have always claimed that they belonged more at work than around the house, many women have recently begun to state the same thing: 'In a previous era, men regularly escaped the house for the bar, the fishing hole, the golf course, the pool hall, or, often enough, the sweet joy of work. Today ... women, ... overloaded and feeling unfairly treated at home, [are] escaping to work, too' (Hochschild, 1997, p. 39). Hochschild's leading concern is the marginalization of life at home, where children must be content with something as strange as 'quality time' and where as many tasks as possible are outsourced.

In her early work, Hochschild appeared in favor of a certain mixing of the worlds of work and home, for permeability between the 'masculine' outside world and the 'all-too-feminine' inside world. In *The Managed Heart* (1983), for example, she criticized the pressure placed on stewardesses to present themselves as something different from what they 'really' were. But in her later work, she argues for a radical separation of work and home, and is extremely ambivalent about the 'feminization of the workplace' ushered in by 'a management philosophy that stressed trust, team building, and courtesy to the internal customer' (Hochschild, 1997, p. 168).

In the United States, where the feminist ambition for women to take an equal part in paid labor is as good as achieved, the problem is that work outside the home has come to dominate the lives of all Americans, men and women alike. The emphasis placed on *family values* in political rhetoric says something about how far removed the ideal has become from the daily reality. Alongside low-paid blue-collar workers, particularly professionals and managers are much too busy (Jacobs and Gerson, 2004a) and *family life* pays the price.

This is the context in which sociologists such as Hochschild, Gornick and Meyers, and Jacobs and Gerson look to Western Europe for solutions. 'Many European countries have adopted programs, such as shorter workweeks, widely available childcare, and generous parental leave policies, that reflect a concern for family welfare and women's rights' (Gerson, 2004b, p. 178). The Netherlands is a good example of the shorter workweek (nowhere in the world do so many men and women have part-time jobs, SCP [2010]), while Norway's highly developed welfare state, with its parental leave schemes for both women and men, is Hochschild's envy: 'In Norway... all employed men are eligible for a year's paternity leave at 90 percent pay. Some 80 percent of Norwegian men now take over a month of parental leave. In this way, Norway is a model to the world' (Hochschild, 2006, p. 219). In *Families that Work: Policies for Reconciling Parenthood and Employment* (2003), sociologists Janet Gornick and Marcia Meyers also look to European countries as models:

> Many of the problems besetting American families are less acute in other industrialized countries that have more extensive public policies that help families manage competing demands from the home and the workplace without sacrificing gender equality. Although none of the countries... can be characterized as having achieved a fully egalitarian, dual-earner-dual-carer society, some provide useful examples of the ways in which government can

support families in their efforts to share earning and caring work. (2003, p. 5)

Gornick and Meyers are also fairly optimistic that gender inequality in the performance of household chores will diminish as European policies are introduced in the US: 'Family policies in several European countries ... provide models of what government can do to help families resolve the tensions between workplace and caring responsibilities while promoting greater gender equality' (2003, p. 15).

This undervaluation of caring responsibilities and private life is at the center of the American debate on the 'crisis of home', in which the main culprits are business, the market and the lack of effective public policy. The assumption is that as part-time work and effective policy ease outside pressures on the family, men will begin to assume their fair share of household and childcare tasks, while women will be able to fulfill their career ambitions. By blaming the state and the market, the attitudes of men largely escape critical attention.[2]

It is from this perspective that Europe, or more precisely certain countries in Northern Europe, appear idyllic. But how accurate is this perception? How equal is the distribution of paid work and caring responsibilities in the lauded European countries of the Netherlands, Sweden and Norway? Do better childcare schemes deliver the promised benefits, and even eliminate the time bind? Do men become better fathers, carers and housekeepers? Do Europeans enjoy a 'true' home?

The Netherlands: the part-time society

The marginalization of family life can be expressed in quantitative terms. The working week of many Americans is long – much longer than the average working week in many European countries, even when we ignore the overtime that many committed employees in the US 'take for granted'. The difference with the Netherlands, the leader in part-time work, is the greatest. It is much more common for Dutch women to work part-time than for American women (75% and 26% respectively) (SCP, 2010; US Department of Labor, 2009): 44.5 percent of Dutch women have a part-time job of 20–34 hours, 15.4 percent work 12–20 hours and 14.6 percent work less than 12 hours a week. Among working Dutch men, 77.1 percent work full time and 22.9 percent part time (12.2% work 20–35 hours a week while 10.8% work less than 20 hours a week) (SCP, 2010).[3]

We would expect that Dutch couples are less likely to suffer from the time bind as they work, on average, considerably fewer hours than their American counterparts. Indeed, for dual-income couples with children, mean joint hours worked per week is 80 in the US and only 61 in the Netherlands (Gornick and Meyers, 2003, p. 61). Of the Dutch couples with children under 18, both men and women worked full time in only 8 percent of cases, one parent worked full time and the other part time in 56 percent, both partners worked part time in 7 percent, and one parent worked full time while the partner had no job in 24 percent of cases. There were also couples where one parent worked part time and one had no job (3%), and others where neither parent had a job (2%). Where one partner worked full time and the second partner had no job, the man was almost always the working parent (SCP, 2010).[4]

It is more difficult to find good data on how Dutch and Americans perceive the time bind. An indication of the more modest dominance of work over home in the Netherlands, however, emerges from interviews among a representative random sample where respondents identify their ambitions and what is most important in their lives. The results suggest that Dutch people are generally unambitious in their work and do not give paid labor a particularly important place in their lives. Only 10 percent of the population considers more than three days of work a week to be ideal for a mother with small children (SCP, 2010). A majority of parents of school-age children consider a two- or three-day working week to be ideal (*ibid.*). To provide some context to this statistic, note that there is less need to demonstrate ambition in the Netherlands by putting in long working hours; almost all households with one and a half incomes can quite easily make ends meet. Data for the US are more ambivalent: 'Some observers…argue Americans work longer hours because they like to work long hours, relative to Europeans' (Gornick and Meyers, 2003, p. 80). Many studies, however, show that the 'choice' to work longer hours is mainly motivated by higher income (Evans *et al.*, 2001). Bell and Freeman conclude that 'in the United States we work hard because we face a good "carrot" for putting out time and effort, and because we also face a substantial "stick" if we do not' (2001, p. 96).

As Gerson puts it: 'The rise of overwork does not reflect worker preferences. ... Instead, it represents a growing mismatch between job demands and reward structures, which equate work commitment with time spent at the workplace' (2004a, p. 55).

'Home' may be more highly valued in the Netherlands than in the United States, but this is mainly because Dutch women make work of home and put private life ahead of their part-time jobs. Some Dutch women do in fact want to work longer hours, but only if certain conditions are met: the most commonly mentioned ones are compatibility of working hours with private life, the ability to take time off for a sick child or family member, and compatibility of working hours with their children's school schedules (SCP, 2010).[5]

Dutch men do little at home compared to women, whether household chores or childcare tasks. Of parents with children up to six years of age, women in 2005 spent 23.7 and 20.7 hours, respectively, on housekeeping and care for children or other household members. The corresponding figures for men were 9.2 and 10 hours. The care tasks of parents with children between six and 14 decline, for both women and men. But there remain significant differences between the sexes: women now spend 24.5 hours per week on housework and 9.4 hours on care, while men spend 9.8 and 3.6 hours respectively (SCP, 2006, p. 106). The fact that women have part-time jobs thus takes the pressure off men to participate at home. In 1995, the total contribution of men to care tasks was 34.9 percent. Ten years later, the situation was virtually unchanged (35.7%). One of the objectives of Dutch emancipation policy – men shouldering at least 40 percent of care obligations by 2010 – has not been achieved.

Dutch men contribute more to housekeeping only when women have more demanding paid jobs. This is interesting, if only because Hochschild appears to follow Harriet Presser in concluding that men's involvement at home does *not* depend on the demands of a woman's paid job: 'when wives go to work outside the home, a third of husbands do more housework and childcare to compensate; a third don't change; and a third actually do less' (Hochschild, 1997, p. 184). While Dutch figures show men assuming more tasks at home as women work more outside (see Tables 3.1 and 3.2), this mechanism mainly operates when men are at home alone with their children: they then have no escape.

Table 3.1 Time spent on paid work/education and housekeeping/care by working people with children (hours per week and percent of time spent on respective tasks)

	Youngest child 0–6 years				Youngest child 7–17 years			
	Women		Men		Women		Men	
	Hours per week	%	Hours per week	%	Hours per week	%	Hours per week	%
The Netherlands								
Paid work/ education	17.7	32	40.7	70	27.8	55	40.7	82
Housekeeping/ care	38.2	68	17.1	30	22.9	45	9.2	18
Total	55.9	100	57.8	100	50.7	100	49.9	100
Sweden								
Paid work/ education	20.0	35	36.9	61	30.7	53	38.1	68
Housekeeping/ care	37.4	65	23.2	39	27.6	47	17.8	38
Total	57.4	100	60.1	100	58.3	100	55.9	100
France								
Paid work/ education	26.6	44	38.5	70	29.5	50	40.4	74
Housekeeping/ care	33.6	56	16.6	30	29.5	50	14.2	26
Total	60.2	100	55.1	100	59.0	100	54.6	100
United States								
Paid work/ education	29.9	47	43.6	69	31.3	54	42.7	74
Housekeeping/ care	34.2	53	19.2	31	26.6	46	14.7	26
Total	64.1	100	62.8	100	57.9	100	57.4	100

Source: SCP (2006).

Table 3.1 below shows that the American hope for a 'more relaxed life' is a reality in the Netherlands, certainly for men. Surveys reveal that Dutch men with children between seven and 17 years of age spend strikingly few hours on housekeeping and care tasks.

At first glance, then, part-time work looks like a good way for households to escape from the time bind. But a closer look at the figures shows that the main reason for this is that Dutch women do little outside the home and much inside. Nowhere else is the proportion of hours spent on housekeeping and childcare as high as it is for Dutch women; nowhere else do men spend so little time on the household and children. In other words, encouraging part-time work when men and women have unequal earning power and sense of 'home responsibility' leads to women spending more time at home – precisely the situation second-wave feminism set out to change.

The Netherlands also shows that while part-time work can bring peace to the home front, it is at the expense of women's careers and economic independence. There is a conspicuous correlation between the proportion of women working part time in the Netherlands and the extremely low proportion of women in more highly qualified jobs. Whereas girls on average are more highly educated than boys, women are greatly under-represented in middle and higher positions. The Netherlands compares poorly in this regard with all other European countries, and certainly with the United States. Only 4.3 percent of board members in the 5,000 largest companies in the Netherlands were women in 2009 (SCP, 2010), compared to more than 15 percent in the US (Catalyst, 2009). Furthermore, only 42 percent of Dutch women between 15 and 64 were considered economically independent in 2008 (CBS, 2010).[6]

Given the situation in the US where around 60 percent of women are financially self-sufficient (Bell, 2010; Bell *et al.*, 2007, p. 17; US Census Bureau, 2010) and more women make it to the top, some American scholars give less weight to the problem of the glass ceiling than to the marginalization of private life. Hochschild writes:

> In the early stages of the women's movement many feminists, myself included, pushed for a restructuring of work life to allow for shorter-hour, flexible jobs and a restructuring of home life so that men would get in on the action. But over the years, this part of the women's movement seems to have surrendered the initiative to feminists more concerned with helping women break through the corporate glass ceiling into long-hours careers. A time movement would have to bring us all back to the question of how

women can become men's equals in a more child-oriented and civic-minded society. (1997, p. 250)

It seems to be one or the other: economic independence and breaking the glass ceiling seem incompatible with a strategy oriented towards part-time work and a more 'child-oriented and civic-minded' lifestyle. A growing number of women have reached the top in the US, where there are few part-time jobs. In the Netherlands, where women in particular work part time, they hit the glass ceiling with a thump (other factors also contribute to Dutch backwardness regarding women at the top, but part-time work certainly plays a significant role). Opting for part-time work has consequences for women's careers. To be more precise, encouraging part-time work without men changing their views on the relative importance of work and home leads to women shouldering (or in the case of the Netherlands, retaining) the lion's share of responsibility for the second shift.

Note that this is not necessarily a case against part-time work, but a warning against encouraging part-time work in a context of gender inequality. Where this inequality does not exist, such as in homosexual relationships, Hochschild's dream appears to be coming true: homosexual couples in the Netherlands where both partners work part time enjoy an egalitarian ideology and also share most household and childcare tasks. But here we need to add a qualifying remark: the group concerned is relatively privileged and highly qualified, and is able to escape the time bind because two part-time incomes are more than sufficient for the household.

Scandinavian welfare states

Hochschild and many other Americans see the Scandinavian countries' generous schemes for leaves of absence (for pregnancy, parenthood and holidays) as the solution for the time bind. As some of these schemes explicitly encourage men to take responsibility at home (Sainsbury, 1999), they should also reduce the double load borne by women. Let us look at the practical consequences of these schemes, starting with their impact on men's participation in childcare and housekeeping in Sweden and Denmark. When we compare their contribution to that of men in other European countries, it indeed seems that Scandinavian men are more involved in childcare (Table 3.2).[7]

Table 3.2   Time spent on paid work and housekeeping/childcare, hours per week (2003)

	Women		Men	
	Paid work	Housekeeping and childcare	Paid work	Housekeeping and childcare
Denmark	36.5	22.4	40.8	13.3
Sweden	37.0	18.9	40.4	13.6
Netherlands	27.4	23.8	39.8	11.6
France	35.9	18.2	40.0	10.4

Source: SCP (2006).

However, if we look at Scandinavian men's involvement in housekeeping, we see that their contribution is not large, and no greater than that of men in other countries such as the United States. This is more surprising if we consider that they have more time (particularly during periods when they are at home more). Scandinavian men do respond to appeals to their fatherhood, and often enjoy caring for their children. However, this does not mean that they also identify with the other aspects of 'home'. Research has shown that Scandinavian men, despite being less affected by the time bind, put their work at the center of their lives just as much as other European and American men. We see no fundamental shift in gender attitudes in the Scandinavian countries (Ellingsaeter, 1999).

The above is not to deny that Scandinavian families suffer less from the time bind than their American counterparts – certainly when the children are young, in life's rush hour (see Table 3.1). But here as well, it is mainly women who spend more time at home. When leave schemes are 'gender neutral', it is mainly women who make use of them; only when regulations specifically and exclusively target men do we see some degree of emancipation. For example, two months of the parental leave in Sweden are exclusively for the father ('use or lose') (Koopmans and Schippers, 2006). But as Seward *et al.* conclude: 'Despite years of encouragement, the most generous paid leave program available, and growing societal support, only in the 1990s did a slight majority of Swedish fathers take at least some of the regular paternal leave' (*ibid.*, 2002, p. 396).

The home-orientation of Scandinavian women does not improve their career prospects (Aisenbrey *et al.*, 2009). Research has shown that generous leave schemes negatively impact on their chances for promotion, if only because women returning to work after a career break gravitate to the public sector (Mandel and Semyonov, 2005, p. 952; Pettit and Hook, 2002). 'The question of gender equality raises vexing concerns in the design of leave policies. Women's disproportionate use of long leaves can result in extended absences from the workplace, exacerbating gender inequality in the home, and gender differentials in paid and unpaid work' (Gornick and Meyers, 2003, p. 101). Indeed, Sweden's labor market is one of the most gender-segregated in the world; women and men occupy jobs traditionally associated with their sex, with women seldom in positions of power (Haas and Hwang, 2007, p. 58).

Both the Dutch solution to the time bind (part-time work) and the Scandinavian one (paid leave) lead to less time pressures because it is women who are more often at home and assume – or continue to accept – the lion's share of both childcare and housekeeping. This is no reason to oppose part-time work or generous leave arrangements. But we may ask whether it is not possible to design schemes for part-time work and leaves of absence such that men, too, can make maximum use of them.

However, European experience points to something more fundamental, unrelated to the *quantitative* lack of time. Even if men – thanks to policy measures American feminist scholars can only dream of – have more time and spend more of it at home, they are reluctant to perform certain tasks. This *qualitative* problem disappears from view in most American analyses as the pressures of the time bind focus attention on both men and women being overburdened by work outside the home. As valuable as this perspective may be, it should not blind us to the fact that women everywhere still assume the lion's share of care tasks, true not only in the US but even more so in part-time paradises like the Netherlands. This is largely because men still do not identify with 'home'.

The greatest merit of the recent work by American sociologists is that it shows how the emancipation of women has taken place on 'male' terms: women have entered the world of paid labor in droves, but this has not been accompanied by the necessary changes that would enable work and care to be combined. Neither have men changed their attitudes towards 'home'. Life at home is thus threatened with marginalization, with many men and women now reporting that they enjoy being at work more than being at home. 'Sadly, many workers felt more appreciated for what they were doing at work than for what they were doing at home' (Hochschild, 2003, p. 207).

Given this situation, Hochschild's strategy to re-evaluate 'home' appears apt. Nevertheless, the European cases show that striving for a more relaxed distribution of work and care through part-time work, more generous leave arrangements and child day care may entail women returning to their former position as the primary home-makers. As necessary as it might be to put the market in its place and make paid labor less dominant in the lives of men and women, progressive social policies by themselves will not usher in the 'new home'. There remains the need for men to re-appreciate 'home'. Otherwise, women will again find themselves confined to the world of 'home' while men continue to identify with the world of 'work'.

Home, what home?

What do people who are so worried about the marginalization of family life in the US really mean by 'home'? We saw in Chapter 2 that 'home' has various meanings, depending on the person, the time and the situation. The question is thus pertinent: according to the authors under discussion here, what kind of 'home' is in crisis?

Whereas second-wave feminists gave some gruesome accounts of the darker sides of 'home as hell', Hochschild in her recent work attaches positive value to home (and to the importance of feeling at home). Precisely because Hochschild sympathizes with many of the ideals of second-wave feminism – so aptly described in *The Second Shift* (1989) as de-romanticizing 'home' – it is interesting to examine her more recent writings, what she means by 'home' and why one should (again) appreciate it.

Hochschild, in her recent writings, stresses the dangers of the decline of home-at-home. She argues that 'one has to feel home at home' and that feelings of home should not become part of 'work' – thus reinstating boundaries she wished to blur in earlier days. Her analysis relies on a rather 'thick' and rosy notion of home – of *home-as-haven*:

> [I assume], as many of us do, that compared to the workplace, home is a more pleasant place to be. ... If the purpose and nature of family and work differ so drastically in our minds, it seemed reasonable to assume that people's emotional experience of the two spheres would differ profoundly, too. In *Haven in a Heartless World*, the social historian Christopher Lasch drew a picture of family as a 'haven' where workers sought refuge after the cruel world of work. (Hochschild, 2003, p. 205)

In 'Emotional Geography and the Flight Plan of Capitalism', Hochschild claims that this positive idea of home applies to both men and women (whereas Lasch's earlier portrait of home-as-haven was taken to task by feminists for its gender bias). Hochschild writes:

> I assumed that working parents would want more time at home. I imagined that they experienced home as a place where they could relax, feel emotionally sheltered and appreciated for who they 'really are.' I imagined home to feel to the weary worker like the place where he or she could take off a uniform, put on a bathrobe, have a beer, exhale... To be sure, home life has its emergencies and strains, but I imagined that home was the place people thought about when they thought about rest, safety, and appreciation. ... The model of family-as-haven led me to assume that the individual would feel most known and appreciated at home and least so at work. (*Ibid.*, pp. 205 and 207)

Hochschild initially seems reluctant to formulate her own ideas about home; instead she elaborates on what she *expects* to hear from the subjects of her research ('I assumed...', 'I imagined...'). Over the course of her research, however, it turns out that many working men and women feel more at home-at-work than at home; home was 'not a haven, a zone of relief and relaxation. It was a workplace' (*ibid.*, p. 206). Somewhat surprisingly, Hochschild is taken aback by women complaining about home in a language reminiscent of second-wave feminism. Even more surprising is Hochschild's criticism of those who feel at home-at-work, on the basis of *her* idea that people should feel more relaxed, sheltered and appreciated at home. Home-as-haven thus turns out to be more her own idea than that of the workers she interviews.

If many people feel unappreciated for what they are doing at home, this may indicate a serious social problem. Indeed, the poor quality of family life as described by Hochschild and many other sociologists indicates severe problems in the lives of American citizens. But why take issue with the trend to make 'work' more like 'home'? Must 'feeling at home' be confined to what we consider the 'private sphere'? Hochschild does not convincingly explain why it is a problem if feelings of home travel, if our homely needs are (also) satisfied in other ways and in other places.

I suppose Hochschild would answer that the undermining of home-at-home is *causally* related to developments at work: people have to invest more hours at work and are willing to do so because work gives them the feeling of being at home. In this way, (post) modern capitalism fuels a vicious circle: due to their jobs, people have less time for their 'real' homes. The situation at home further deteriorates, and people are happy to escape to work where they can finally experience the feeling of home. Hochschild claims that this is against the will of both women and men. If they could choose to feel at home at home, they would. For Hochschild, unrestrained market capitalism is the root cause of the American crisis of home. The market is for her the most improbable sphere for feeling at home.

I fully agree with Hochschild that the US is experiencing a much more serious crisis of home-at-home than most West European countries. Placing restrictions on the free market, improving welfare state entitlements and encouraging part-time work would indeed reduce the pressure American households experience today. But note what, for Hochschild, constitutes a 'good' home when she writes: 'Four-year-old Cassie, waiting to be picked up at the Spotted Deer Childcare Center, will have passed through a childhood of long waits for absent parents' (Hochschild, 1997, pp. 258–9). Is a four-year-old attending day care here seen as a problem? Cassie is missing her parents, missing a real home, implying that even the Scandinavian solution falls short. The point here is not whether Hochschild is right regarding what children need. The point is that the 'thicker' one's notion of home – of what must be done to provide a 'real' one – the more it will burden women. Even under Scandinavian conditions, most men refuse to identify with home; the main reason family life is faring better in countries like the Netherlands is because women continue to do the unpaid work.

Dalton Conley in his book on home and work, *Elsewhere, USA* (2009), proposes a radically different solution. His is a very thin notion of home:

> Successful companies ... in the coming years will be the ones who – like Google – blend and bend rather than build walls between the domains of life. For example, rather than drop-off day care, a new model called 'Two rooms' offers office space for working parents separated only by glass from their toddlers, who explore a play space in the next room. The *kinder* are supervised by an adult, but the parents and the children can wave, signal each other, and cross the divide as often as they want in between their respective block-towers and e-mail messages. ... The professional parents will be the ones who manage to blend the child-rearing duties with their professional ones, making their children comfortable in high-pressure, high-status work environments where big vocabulary words fly back and forth and the kids get used to the 'family business,' so to speak. (p. 183)

For Conley, the crisis of home in the United States will be solved when work and home ultimately fuse:

> It's that the once disparate spheres have now collided and inter-penetrated each other, creating a sense of 'elsewhere' at all times. I'm not just talking about the increase in travel and telecommunications, I am talking about the more subtle changes that they have rendered: the fact that home is more like work and work is more like home and that the private and public spheres are increasingly indistinguishable from each other. (*Ibid.*, p. 33)

Conley further argues that 'we shouldn't try to swim against the tides of history in our own lives' (*ibid.*, p. 183) – implying that the dissolution of the private 'home-at-home' is inevitable.

That the 'tides of history' have put an end to the idea of *home-as-haven* can be questioned on both empirical and normative grounds. Would Conley's way out really solve the crisis of home in America?

And for whom? Would it address the problems of people with (very) low-paid jobs, who now often combine two or more of them? Conley, in his book, does not elaborate on the many consequences of his radical proposal.

Conley's argument, however, has the benefit of showing that there are more possible answers to the American crisis of home than Hochschild's *home-as-haven* (a place that needs to be protected from the world). Yet another strategy is sketched by Dolores Hayden in *Redesigning the American Dream: Gender, Housing, and Family Life*: the 'neighborhood' strategy of home-making where 'home' is no longer a trap as better designed houses and shared services 'overcome the isolation of housewives' (2002, p. 108).

When thinking about possibilities for the future, we need to realize that both the old and new ideals of home are deeply inter-twined with notions of gender. The very idea of home–as-haven was based on a new role for women, at least for middle-class women. Tamara Hareven, the late family historian, has shown that the 'concept of the home as the family's haven and domestic retreat emerged ... about one hundred fifty years ago, and was, initially, lim-ited to the urban middle classes' (1993, p. 228). In earlier days – as has also been shown by French historian Philip Aries – the notion of 'privacy' did not apply to 'home': 'In preindustrial society the family conducted its work and public affairs *inside* the household' (*ibid.*, p. 230). Industrialization and urbanization fueled the idea of the *home-as-haven* in highly gendered terms (Chapman and Hockey, 1999; Massey, 2007):

> The view of the home as the family's private retreat was closely linked to the new definition of woman's separate sphere, which glorified the role of the wife as a homemaker and full-time mother. In American society, the cult of domesticity that characterized this transformation in women's roles placed women on a pedes-tal as the custodians of the home and segregated them in their domestic sphere, while the public sphere was allotted exclusively to men. (Massey, 2007, pp. 237–8)

All this implies that 'the division between domestic and work-spaces and relations between the private and public realms, was never as neat as the home as haven idea implies' (Mallet, 2004, p. 72). An invention of the nineteenth century, the strict boundary between 'home' and 'work' – and between the 'private' and 'public' – was in the second half of the twentieth century criticized particularly by women for its unfair gender implications. This led to new ideas about home, more in line with what I have called *home-as-heaven*. No longer a refuge from the outside world, the new home would aid self-actualization and reaching out to the world. The boundaries between private and public were blurred, not least because 'the public' became a place where people could feel at home as well. 'While the idea of home, as a retreat or withdrawal from public spaces, continues to be appealing, it is now matched by a move in the other direction: taking the home into the public sphere, domesticating the public sphere' (Kumar and Makarova, 2008, p. 332).

To be fair, Hochschild recognizes the importance of home's outward-orientation when she emphasizes the importance of civic-mindedness. Her defense of *home-as-haven* is primarily meant to defend it from the market, not civil society. On the other hand, Conley stretches home's outward-orientation to its limits: his book can be read as a radical plea for the incorporation of 'home' in the economic sphere.

The authors cited here all agree that a new relationship is developing between the public and private spheres (mostly understood here in terms of 'work' and 'home'). All also agree that family life is under siege in the US. The crisis of home will be the subject of heated debate for years to come: at stake is the role of government, employers, employees, citizens and members of households. Should we swim with 'the tide of history' or try to turn it? Conley swims (and sinks 'home' as a meaningful ideal): in his book he promises his wife that he will no longer shout at her for trying to involve the kids in her professional life, or to turn off her cell phone during 'family time' (Conley, 2009, p. 206). Hochschild's agenda is much more ambitious: it includes a more prominent government role in social welfare and a fundamental change in men's attitudes towards home. As long as these two don't happen, the American crisis at home will continue.

4
New Ways of Home-making: Feeling at Home in the Community?

Introduction

On the basis of the last chapter, one may wonder if 'home' is nothing more than a *topos* loaded with nostalgia. But though there is, in the US, a strong longing for the past regarding home-at-home, there is more to home today than nostalgia; we also see conscious efforts at home-making for a better future. This chapter focuses on two social movements explicitly striving for new homes at the community level.

The first is the movement fighting for the interests of people with psychiatric and intellectual disabilities. Its participants favor *community care* where patients can find their place among 'normal' people rather than being isolated in institutions. Societal discrimination – resulting in people living as outcasts – should, in their view, be countered by caring communities.

The second example concerns gays and lesbians. As their family members often rejected their sexual identity, gays and lesbians had to look for places that would feel more like home. In their quest, they often gravitated to the big cities where anonymity allowed invisibility and where they could meet other gays and lesbians for relationships, sexual excitement and safe social lives. Metropolitan conditions favored the gathering of like-minded individuals, creating possibilities for public gay communities.

For both gays and lesbians and people with psychiatric and intellectual disabilities, home often resembled 'hell': discrimination either pushed them out of their family homes (gays and lesbians) or locked them in 'total institutions' (people with intellectual disabilities). Social movements thus began to campaign for new places that would feel like home. This chapter examines these new home-making practices in which a warm and connecting community was to replace the coldness and/or isolation of their former homes.

While the previous chapter dealt with developments at the level of the household, this chapter explicitly focuses on the meso level of communities, defined as 'dense, multiplex, relatively autonomous networks of social relationships. Community, thus, is not a place or simply a small-scale population aggregate, but a mode of relating, variable in extent' (Calhoun, 1998, p. 391). As we will see, new home-making practices at the community level were less successful for the mentally handicapped than for gays. As it turned out, people with psychiatric and intellectual disabilities did not move from institutions into welcoming communities ('heaven', where they could lead public or semi-public lives); they instead moved into small, independent housing units ('havenly' places that were safe, secure, comfortable and private). While independent housing was an improvement, it was not the type of new home that the caring community movement had aspired to. The home-making practices of gays, in contrast, were more communal: they organized public places that had elements of 'heaven', thus providing identity and visibility to their community.

From hell to haven: home-making by people with psychiatric and intellectual disabilities

In many Western countries, the past 25 years have witnessed a policy of de-institutionalization for psychiatric patients and people with intellectual disabilities. No longer banished to countryside institutions, de-institutionalization posited that it would be better for these people to once again be a part of society, to live in ordinary neighborhoods in towns and villages. While there would be additional support, the idea was that individuals would live in their own houses as autonomously as possible. Since the late 1990s, this policy has broadly been referred to as *community care*.

Prior to the 1970s, psychiatric patients and people with intellectual disabilities were viewed as people in need of continuous nursing and tucked away in countryside institutions. The therapeutic ideal prescribed that the best place to care for them was in large institutions far away from their former daily environments. Patients could be cared for and supervised 24 hours a day; here they would find peace and quiet, ample space and a well-regulated life. In the 1970s, patient organizations as well as professionals and academics began to criticize this 'medical regime', asserting that remote institutions only served to isolate people from 'normal' communities. Institutions were not only deemed discriminatory; they failed to make people less ill or disturbed.

Asylums: Essays on the Social Situation of Mental Patients and Other Inmates (1961), the iconic work by the American sociologist Erving Goffman, was a source of inspiration for the critics of institutionalization. Goffman compared psychiatric hospitals to other 'total institutions' such as prisons, barracks, convents and even concentration camps. Their 'total' nature was embodied in barriers such as locked doors, high walls, electric fences, water and woodland that precluded contact with the outside world. For Goffman, another feature of the total institution was that work, sleep and leisure were group events – in the same location, regulated by a strict schedule, and under the same bureaucratic regime. The worst feature of the asylum was that the inmate's 'self is systematically, if often unintentionally, mortified' (Goffman, 1961, p. 15).

Goffman and other influential critics, including the psychiatrists Ronald Laing (1960) and Thomas Szasz (1961), argued that it was not so much institutionalized inmates who were ill or mad, as society itself. It was society that made people ill. And to make society healthy, psychiatric patients and people with intellectual disabilities had a role to play. Their presence would confront 'normal' people with the vulnerable aspects of their own existence and make society more humane (Tonkens, 1999).

The Swedish social scientist Bengt Nirjé was one of the first to argue that people with intellectual disabilities should lead 'normal lives': 'The normalization principle means making available to all mentally retarded people patterns of life and conditions of everyday living which are as close as possible to the regular circumstances and ways of life of society' (Nirjé, 1969, p. 179). It entailed participating in education, housing, work and having social contacts in society.

In the Netherlands this new thinking was encapsulated in the policies of Nieuw Dennendal, an institution for people with intellectual disabilities which became famous in the 1970s for its progressive approach. The spontaneous development of the self was central to its philosophy of care: clients were free to discover their own talents and potential, while society merely had the task of supporting this. The policies of the Nieuw Dennendal reflected the ideal of the late 1970s that not only tolerated deviant behavior, but saw it as a healthy reaction to a sick society (Duyvendak, 1999). It was therefore also in the interests of society that psychiatric patients and people with mental disabilities would come to feel at home in society.

The era of de-institutionalization

Policy-makers were surprisingly responsive to the criticism embodied in the new thinking: they introduced a policy of de-institutionalization, offering extramural support and treatment for patients who needed long-term care but who no longer lived in residential institutions (Kwekkeboom, 2004; Means and Smith, 1998; Overkamp, 2000; Welshman, 2006). Several Western countries (the UK, Italy and the Scandinavian countries) closed down many psychiatric hospitals and institutions, replacing them with small facilities in ordinary communities providing local extramural care. Norway and Sweden introduced legislation that entitled anyone with any kind of disability to live in a house in an ordinary neighborhood; in fact, patients had no choice as these countries no longer maintained residential institutions. In the US, financial considerations prevailed: when state governments realized that de-institutionalization could save money, they embraced the idea. But as they often did not provide sufficient funding for smaller facilities, large numbers of the mentally ill ended up homeless on the streets.

In the Netherlands, policy-makers interpreted the criticism of institutions mainly as one of scale and type of housing: the size and impersonal nature of the institutions were thus consigned to the past as 'small' became the maxim of the 1980s and 1990s. Small-scale sheltered living units were established, first in the grounds of institutions, and later, beyond the institutions' confines in residential neighborhoods in towns and villages (Means and Smith, 1998; Overkamp, 2000; Welshman, 2006). The 1984 'New Memorandum on the Mental Health Service' explicitly stated that the closed, large-scale approach to institutional mental healthcare was to be replaced by a care system 'in which the client can be helped close to his home, maintaining his social contacts as far as possible' (Dutch Parliament [Tweede Kamer], 1983/1984, p. 53). The number of beds in psychiatric institutions was to be reduced, while some of the released funds were to be spent on extramural care for these patients in the form of ambulatory care and sheltered living schemes. While these policy changes were responses to criticisms, they were also prompted by the need to restrain mental healthcare expenditure. Other Dutch policy documents in the 1990s expanded on the theme of de-institutionalization. The maxim of the memorandum 'In the Community: Mental Health and Mental Healthcare in a Social Perspective' was 'mental healthcare (back) in the community where possible' (Dutch Parliament [Tweede Kamer], 1992/1993, p. 76). A 'community-based concept of care' was central to this approach, to be achieved by mental healthcare services cooperating at the local level with social services, homeless centers, legal services and employment and social rehabilitation projects.

Dutch care policies for people with intellectual disabilities evolved in a similar fashion. The new policy stated: 'First and foremost, the disabled must be given more freedom to make their own choices about how they lead their lives' (VWS, 1995, p. 16). 'Living in an ordinary house in an ordinary neighborhood' (*ibid.*, p. 43) became the guiding principle. Once again – as was the case with the mental health service – the need to curb expenditure was an additional argument in favor of de-institutionalization.

However, policy documents from the late 1990s (Dutch Parliament [Tweede Kamer], 1996/1997, 1998/1999) indicate that the switch to community care did not develop according to plan. Although normalizing the position of psychiatric patients and people with intellectual disabilities remained the aim, there were indications that the process of de-institutionalization was not fulfilling its goals. According to the Minister of Health, Welfare and Sport, Els Borst, there were signs that community care was negatively influencing the quality of life of those handicapped people who had begun living on their own. The minister also observed that care institutions were still not investing enough in extramural help and support, and that cooperation with local partners was unsatisfactory. Reducing levels of institutional care could only be justified if it was replaced by social support functions in the community. 'Experience in other countries has demonstrated that without this support, the move to mental healthcare in the community can lead to the exclusion, decline and increasing isolation of patients' (Dutch Parliament [Tweede Kamer], 1996/1997, p. 10).

Although politicians maintained reservations about the effects of community care, they only strengthened their policy that people with handicaps should not rely on services and amenities for their specific disabilities, but should – where possible – use those available to the general public. In 2007 this policy was explicitly formulated in a new law on social support, the central concept of which was 'participation'. Everyone was supposed to participate in society; those who for whatever reason were unable to participate on their own were entitled to the support of their social networks, neighbors, volunteers and, in the last resort, professionals. The new law applied to psychiatric patients and the intellectually disabled as well, people for whom being a part of the 'normal' community entailed a great deal of special help and support. The question thus became poignant: are all neighbors and neighborhoods willing and able to provide this help?

Having your own home

My research team interviewed about 100 people with psychiatric problems or intellectual disabilities living on their own in 'normal' Dutch neighborhoods. Most of the interviewed psychiatric patients had spent considerable periods of their lives in psychiatric hospitals. Of the respondents with intellectual disabilities, half had previously lived in institutions run by professionals; the others had lived with their parents. Respondents all stated that they had chosen to live on their own; none felt obliged or forced by relatives or professionals to choose this option. Most received a house in the town where they had grown up. About half had a lease in their own name; others leased via the care organization that supported them. Respondents had no explicit expectations about how it would be to live on their own, nor any definite expectations about their new neighborhoods – for instance, whether they would feel welcome or if their neighbors would help them settle in.

Respondents unanimously appreciated having their own houses where they could do what they wanted: 'Once you are free in your own house, that's really terrific. ... Even when the weather is bad, it still seems as if the sun is shining. That's my feeling here' (man with intellectual disabilities, 30). They mentioned advantages such as not being constantly disturbed by others, being in control of what and when they eat, their bedtimes, pets in the house, having more autonomy, etc.: 'Finally I am in control over the remote control.' No one wanted to return to their former living condition.

> I decided that it was enough with all those non-stop intakes in hospital. I really wanted to have a life in a place of my own. And here I am now: I am really calmer now that I am not continuously in and out of the institution and don't have to live in a group anymore. I have the tendency to adjust myself always to other people around me and I'm happy now that it's not necessary anymore. (Woman, 45, psychiatric patient)

> For many years I lived in institutions with a lot of people constantly around me. But it is no good for me to be with so many people all the time, because my head becomes too busy then. Maybe I get mad one day. That's why I have asked for a home of my own. And finally that worked out fine, because now I live here on my own and I like that very much. (Man with intellectual disabilities, 33)

Other researchers (e.g., Kwekkeboom, 2006; Kwekkeboom and van Weert, 2008; Overkamp, 2000) have also concluded that most individuals with psychiatric problems or intellectual disabilities prefer to have their own accommodation, due to the privacy and autonomy this allows. They opt for homes that have 'haven' qualities: secure, safe, comfortable and private. In this respect, their lives have undoubtedly improved.

At home in the community?

In general, our interviewees had very little, if any, contact with neighbors or other locals in their new neighborhoods. Most did not introduce themselves after they moved in; nor did supporting professionals suggest they do so. Only one respondent, a 60-year old man with psychiatric problems, explicitly told us about his attempt to make contact with his neighbors:

> Shortly after I moved in I called on the neighbors around ten in the evening. I said I'd just wanted to pop in for a drink, but they

said: 'Sorry, it's far too late, not now'. Next day those neighbors complained to the care institution that I was a nuisance. So my contact with the neighbors was not much of a success.

Contact with neighbors was usually limited to saying hello and, at best, to brief chats on the street. There was very little deeper contact – for example, drinking coffee together or helping each other with small tasks. Some interviewees mentioned unpleasant experiences with neighbors. A 31-year-old woman with intellectual disabilities told us that, not long after her move, she found bits of food on her doormat that had been stuffed through the letterbox. This happened at least five times. She was quite sure that it was one of her neighbors.

Those who visited our interviewees in their homes were mainly relatives and personal carers. Respondents looked forward to their daily or weekly visits when they could talk about what was going on in their lives. In many cases the carer was often called 'the most important person in my life'. Beyond this, contact was generally limited to people in similar positions as themselves. They met each other at work (most often for people with handicaps), in the activity center (most often for people with the same handicap), or at the meeting place of the care organization. For many interviewees the latter functioned as a living room, a place to easily chat with others. In this sense, these places were, like their homes, 'safe havens'.

Few respondents enjoyed friendly contacts with 'normal' people. Several interviewees mentioned feelings like shyness, uncertainty and even fear:

I feel more secure when I am with people like myself. Everywhere else I don't feel at ease. People look at you as if they think: What is he doing here? (Man with intellectual disabilities, 30)

Most normal people think you're not right in the head, so they don't want to have anything to do with you. I suppose that is discrimination. Or maybe not discrimination, but prejudice. Or even fear, maybe they're just scared. (Woman, 48, psychiatric patient)

Look here, I'm someone with slight intellectual disabilities. I can stand up for myself, but you're never sure if normal people make a fool of you. (Woman with intellectual disabilities, 39)

The same fears of not being able to keep up with 'normal' people, and of being nagged or stigmatized, meant most interviewees didn't visit the community center or attend other public activities in their neighborhoods.

> Two or three times I visited the community center here, but I didn't feel happy there. There's more distance and coolness than in the DAC [the activity center for people with psychiatric problems]. Everyone comes there, maybe even your neighbors, you never know. That's a real threshold for me. That's why I prefer to go to the DAC. There I feel at home and there I'm not the only one who is seen as mad, because there are others who have also experienced a psychosis. (Woman, 52, psychiatric patient)

Although respondents' social networks were generally small, this did not necessarily mean that they were dissatisfied with them. About 65 percent of interviewees thought their networks were sufficient. This applied mainly to those who still lived in the neighborhood or in the part of town where they had grown up, with nearby relatives frequently dropping in to help with small tasks. Some respondents even mentioned incidental contacts with one or more former classmates. The subgroup of respondents satisfied with their social networks also included individuals, mainly those with psychiatric problems, who hardly saw other people. This 44-year-old woman was typical:

> I live here quietly; the heath is nearby. I like it here, the trees too. Because of my psychiatric problems I'm not allowed to work. My days have a simple structure: in the morning I take out my dog, make some coffee and after that I watch TV with a cigarette. Well, at those moments I sit like a prince in my chair. In the afternoon I take a nap and after that I take the dog out again. And in the evening I go with the dog for the third time. I don't cook anymore, I don't like it. I just eat bread every day. My family is far away; only my mother lives nearby. She is already 90 years old. Every Saturday evening we visit each other; one week I go to her place, the other week she comes to me. Once in two weeks someone from the care organization comes along. I barely go outdoors, only for the shopping and with the dog. When I take the dog out I often see a man

with another dog. We have a short chat now and then. Apart from my mother, the carer and the man with the dog, I don't see other people. I'm a bit like a hermit, but that's what I want. Sometimes I feel lonely, then I listen to a nice CD and that helps a bit. I'm just not someone who gets really involved in things. A few years ago I tried fitness and I also had a buddy, but I can't commit myself. After a while I just want to be at home: in my chair, with my dog and a cigarette. Then I'm fine.

Most respondents belonging to the 35 percent who were dissatisfied with their social networks lived in environments that were relatively new to them, without family or former acquaintances in the neighborhood. They longed for more contacts but were simply unable to make or maintain them. For these people, personal carers were crucial. The story of a 46-year-old man with intellectual disabilities was illustrative: he told us he never had visitors apart from his carer and mother. This was why he was willing to be interviewed – he would have a visitor! He often felt lonely; each time he did he would count to ten and back several times, which helped him calm down. Though he is pleased with his own home and independence, he misses a 'friendly, sociable atmosphere' in his neighborhood. When asked if he had ever initiated a conversation with anyone, he replied that he would be unlikely to do so because his immediate neighbors had gossiped about him.

Individuals with intellectual disabilities tended more often than people with psychiatric disorders to have structured daily routines they are happy with: four or five days a week they go to the sheltered employment service or to other day-care centers in the neighborhood where they can meet their peers. Psychiatric patients generally found it more difficult to stick to a structured daily or weekly routine. The very nature of their disorder means they tend to be more emotionally unstable; they may suffer mood swings or feel inactive due to medication, making it difficult to maintain social contacts. One woman, when asked if she would like to get to know more people in the neighborhood, replied:

No, not at the moment. It's my head – having to cope with lots of different people is very, very tiring. It's not that I don't like it, it's just that I find things really difficult. My head makes me feel like a stranger in my own body, so I don't really feel at ease anywhere. Not even in my own home. I can't get to the real me, can you understand that? Things wouldn't be OK for me even if I lived in heaven, simply because it's a feeling I have inside me. (Woman with psychiatric problems, 37)

Feeling at home

We asked our interviewees where and to what extent they felt at home, and whether they felt they belonged in their new neighborhoods. Many immediately began to point around them, indicating that they felt at home in their own houses. Here they had rediscovered a place for themselves, free of disturbances, after having lived in groups for many years in different types of institutions. As for the neighborhood, most respondents did not mention definite feelings of attachment. For the reasons outlined above, the neighborhood for most of them had little meaning. They did not know their neighbors; nor did they participate in the life of the neighborhood. Only in cases where they were born and raised in the immediate area did respondents experience an attachment to their environment that resembled a sense of belonging.

The people we interviewed clearly saw their home as a *haven*, a place associated with safety, security, comfort, domesticity and intimacy. Whereas policy-makers tend to privilege the view of home-as-*heaven* – the community as a warm bath where psychiatric patients and people with intellectual disabilities can publicly be themselves – many members of these groups only experience a feeling of belonging when they feel safe and secure, when they are with people like themselves, and when they are in familiar surroundings. It is this last aspect they have difficulty achieving, as they do not manage to establish meaningful contacts with neighbors and other locals.

Conclusion

The majority of the psychiatric patients and people with intellectual disabilities we interviewed live as solitary individuals in their communities (or on isolated 'islands' in the case of clustered accommodation). Pleased with their newfound autonomy, our respondents felt at home in their own houses. In terms of Table 1.2, they belong to the group of relatively immobile people for whom their 'house is home' – 'defensive localists' surrounded by their own, specific goods but out of touch with the outside world. The location of their houses is of limited relevance as they have little or no contact with other locals. To put it bluntly, their neighbors don't care for them and they don't care for the neighborhood. The outside world penetrates their houses almost exclusively via television, for here they can control the remote control – the outside world at a distance.

In retrospect, it is surprising that in the planning of de-institutionalization, so little attention was paid to the social context in which former inmates would end up living. In the 1970s, the idealistic critics of total institutions assumed that society as a whole would benefit from the arrival in local communities of psychiatric patients and people with intellectual disabilities, and vice versa. While policy-makers in the 1980s and 1990s rated highly the benefits of living in a normal house in a normal area, they failed to perceive what this would entail for the everyday lives of those involved. They failed to question whether society as a whole, and more specifically neighborhoods, would show sufficient tolerance and solidarity for vulnerable people; living independently in the community had become an indisputable principle. Professionals and policy-makers have only recently realized that a social network in the immediate neighborhood is crucial for individuals with limited mobility. Policy-makers thus envisioned new communal homes for the handicapped (home-as-heaven) without thinking about the conditions that had to be fulfilled to lead such lives. But if the handicapped are to truly feel at home in the community – being and expressing themselves in public, etc. – mainstream communities will have to change significantly to accommodate this minority.

Recent research in the Netherlands has examined how local communities experience psychiatric patients and people with intellectual disabilities coming to live among them (Kwekkeboom, 1999, 2001; Overkamp, 2000). While reactions to their arrival are at first fairly positive, residents, when questioned further, tend to be less open-minded. Many think there should always be a carer on hand 'just in case', and are reluctant to allow the newcomers into their private lives. This reluctance to include was found among all social strata; psychiatric patients and people with intellectual disabilities were just not considered 'normal' neighbors, contradicting the optimism of both movement activists and policy-makers. No wonder that, in practice, home-as-haven has prevailed over home-as-heaven.

From hell to heaven: moving to the Castro, a gay neighborhood in the making

In homophobic societies, many adolescents who develop same-sex preferences want to leave their 'hometowns' in order to escape from fights with their families. Especially when they enter same-sex relationships, young gays are quite often literally pushed away from the house and community of origin and drawn to inner-city areas (Rosenfeld and Byung-Soo, 2005, p. 559). As they leave the places of their birth and childhood in search of new homes, many gays and lesbians experience a strong sense of uprootedness. In the United States, where negative views of homosexuality were rampant until the late 1990s, gay men and lesbians born in the Mid-West often escaped to cities considered safe havens, such as New York and San Francisco. Forced to leave their hometowns in order to feel free, to find their true selves and to meet others with the same sexual preference, their move to these cities often had, in those days, a non-voluntary character. Since home was not home to them, their 'coming out' in the Castro was often framed in terms of 'coming home'. Traveling to a new place finally provided the opportunity to act out their sexual selves.

Since gay places are almost never starting points but places of arrival, the question arises how these places are valued. Most research shows that gay men and lesbian women often embraced their newfound places; the Castro, San Francisco's gay neighborhood, was often described as a Mecca. 'In San Francisco, we're the world, as much as anybody is. ... You get up in the morning and go out and live in it. Stores, papers, billboards, people on the street, everywhere you fucking look. ... Bite down: It's there. ... Hey: It's home' (Tate, 1991, p. 276). But some, although they preferred the Castro to the places they had left, felt trapped, homesick and angry at having had to leave. Living in the gay Mecca thus turned out to be an ambivalent experience that didn't live up to all expectations (Preston, 1991, p. xiv). And while many gays and lesbians expressed affection for their new place of residence, it was not an easy love; the Castro was also celebrated because there were few alternatives. But the fact that the number of possible destinations was extremely limited did not temper the sense of belonging; in fact it strengthened it.

Put differently, attachments to gay neighborhoods are the result of complex relations between social marginality and geographical (im)mobility. Below, after reconstructing how these places came into being, I examine the changing meanings gay men ascribe to the Castro, the extent to which they consider the neighborhood their home, and how they discursively construct and visually display their public, 'heavenly' sense of home to the outside world. I most often refer to gay men – and less to lesbian women – since my own research has mainly focused on gay men and their feelings of belonging.

Mobility and marginality: where do they come from, where do they go?

The process of gay men moving from traditional rural communities to inner-city neighborhoods is informed by both push and pull factors. 'There was no way for a gay man to have a hometown and still be honest with himself,' Preston writes. 'He had to hide his social and sexual proclivities, or else he had to give up communal life in pursuit of them' (*ibid.*, p. xii). Preston's claim has been corroborated. In their analysis of geographical mobility among gays in the US, Rosenfeld and Bryung-Soo (2005) show that interracial gay couples are the most mobile social group, followed by same-race same-sex couples, interracial heterosexual couples and, finally, same-race heterosexual couples. Individuals within transgressive types of sexual union are thus geographically more mobile than 'traditional' couples (*ibid.*, p. 559). 'While the majority of young adults in traditional unions are more likely to settle near their communities of origin, the small but rising number of young US-born adults in non-traditional unions have been using educational opportunities and open labor markets to put physical and social distance between themselves and their communities of origin' (*ibid.*, p. 549). The research has shown that these patterns of geographical mobility can be seen everywhere in the Mid-West (*ibid.*, p. 555).

Historians have reconstructed how San Francisco developed into a Mecca for gay men and lesbians. The city's reputation as an open frontier, dating from the early twentieth century but finding contemporary embodiment in its bohemian and queer quarters, attracted adventurous pleasure seekers as well as individuals and families looking for a better life. Especially during the 1950s and 1960s, San Francisco's reputation as a place for nonconformist sexual lifestyles fueled its image as a gay capital (Boyd, 1997, pp. 88–9). The media played an important role in this, perpetuating the image of gay life as a geographically fixed phenomenon (Meeker, 2006, pp. 190–1). Books played a similar role (*ibid.*, p. 67). 'I've decided that I must remove myself to another environment where I would have ample opportunity to meet other homosexuals and lead a new life as I want to lead it,' wrote a gay man in a 1964 letter. 'Accordingly to an article in the June 26th issue of *Life Magazine*, titled "Homosexuality in America," the city of San Francisco is the "gay capital" of this country. I feel that this is the place for me' (cited in *ibid.*, p. 181).

San Francisco's emergence as a Mecca for gays and lesbians, both to live in and to visit as tourists, does not mean that they were the sole carriers of this development. Boyd (2003), for example, stresses the role of the tourist economy. A leading source of income for the city, tourism to San Francisco in large part depended on the city's libertine image (Boyd, 1997, p. 85). 'Although gay and gender-transgressive bars and taverns emerged in San Francisco's post-Prohibition era as vulnerable and highly contested public spaces, they continued to function visibly as part of an urban economy of highly trafficked sex tourism' (*ibid.*). The mainstream media's growing attention to homosexual life further enabled many gay men and lesbians to imagine a place that could become home.

Although this is not the place for a detailed history of the Castro (for this see Armstrong, 2002; Leyland, 2002; Stryker and van Buskirk, 1996), I can point out that as the Castro turned into a gay community in the late 1960s, many gays and lesbians expressed a pronounced sense of neighborhood pride. It was the home of the yearly Gay Parade, the Castro Fair, Halloween and other public events that showcased how gays and lesbians loved to live in the Castro. Gay men's and lesbians' identification with the Castro-as-home was reinforced by the naming of distinctive restaurants and cafes such as *Home* and *Welcome Home* (see pictures). Many gays and lesbians, indeed considered the Castro as an ideal place to live – in a word *heaven*. They experienced moving to the Castro as an escape from *hell*, and felt they could now stop dreaming about a better place.

The public visibility of homosexuality marked the quintessence of the Castro as a nonconformist place to live and work. Since hiding one's sexuality was what almost all gay men and lesbian women had

done before coming to the Castro, to 'come out' – both to each other and to the homophobic outside world – became the cornerstone of a newly acquired identity. 'Being oneself' was not something to be lived individually or to be confined to the private sphere: their new home was not a haven, but *heaven*.

The Castro: resisting the generic, becoming the symbolic?

In a sense, the Castro became a new home because it embodied the very opposite of the places gays and lesbians had left behind. By proudly affirming their identity, they challenged the norms and family values of the 'other' America. The social mobilization of gay men (here I focus mostly on gay men) in the Castro centered around the burning wish to feel, be and act differently – and to be respected. In terms of Chapter 1, gay men considered the Castro a *particular* place to be defended against invasions of the *generic*. For example, in October 1999 an initiative called 'Save the Castro' mobilized against the arrival of a Starbucks and the extension of the cable car F-line to the neighborhood. Protests against these developments revealed a distinctive line of argumentation, as can be seen in the following statement titled 'A Kind of War':

> There is a war going on in our neighborhood. It is a war for your dollars and businesses. Every time you shop at one of the new Chains stores, you take away business from local merchant owned shops and restaurants. *Starbucks is symbolic* of the kind of mega-corporation that buys up other chains and squeezes out competition. *They are the McDonalds of coffee and are a part of anyplace USA.* The Castro is unique in the world. (Save the Castro, emphasis in original)

The consequences of the cable car extension were depicted in the same way:

> It is possible that millions of people will be coming to this district very shortly, on these 'historic cars', designed we think to lure tourists onto them. ... *The problem is that this is the only neighborhood like it in the world.* The Castro has a kind of 'mythic regard' overseas, and we are the 'guardians' of this place for future generations. (Save the Castro, emphasis in original)

The above makes it clear that for some gay residents, the outside world was to remain outside. Interestingly, the author appeals to an *ethos of solidarity* among gay men in San Francisco, not by emphasizing the local and rooted character of the Castro but by putting their struggle in a universal perspective. Only if the Castro remains theirs will gay men worldwide be able to consider the district as their home. Ron Wiggin, organizer of the 'Save the Castro' project, warns in a letter to his critics that this sense of home could easily disappear:

> And if the Castro fades under the throngs of tourists from the not needed historic trolley car ... and the rents go up more and the condemning attitudes of the out-of-towners coming walking down our streets, and the stores change to sell to them, and we don't want to go there anymore because we don't feel comfortable. (1991)

The nonconformism was colored by a romanticization of life on the margins, a sense of being different and special, even better than the straight world. However, a close reading shows that – as is often the case – the norms of the margins betray the margins of normality (Duyvendak, 1997). Mobilization on behalf of a 'special' gay community sometimes echoed the tight-knit, rural communities most gay men came from; the small, safe, homogeneous world they wanted to protect in a way reflected the world of their own pasts. Their rejection of mainstream and generic America was at least partly due to their deep desire to be rooted, a longing gay men shared with many others.

One of the critics of the 'Save the Castro' initiative, Vince Quackenbush, attacked this desire to keep others out. Proclaiming the need to 'save the Castro from saving the Castro', he warned gays against barricading themselves in a safe haven for themselves, an unwelcoming community for others. 'The Castro Neighborhood Council is a self-appointed rump group which views change in the Castro as threatening. Instead of seeing the Castro as a base from which queer liberation can flow, "Save the Castro" views our neighborhood as a cocoon-like ghetto that achieved perfection in 1979' (Quackenbush, 1999). Similar critiques were directed against gay activists embracing a 'ghettoized consciousness':

> There are many things wrong with the Castro ... They have a *shtetl* consciousness – you know, like the Jewish ghetto. They patronize

Castro Street businesses; in fact, they seldom leave the area. It's like the man who went to the local Jewish tailor and later reported, 'You get a bad suit but lots of conversation' (Cited in White, 1980, p. 38)

Core elements of the critique address the inward-orientation of the gay community and the uniformity of its members. The desire to be the antithesis of mainstream society, to create a communal front, has given birth to 'the Castro clone' (cf. the 'Chelsea boy' in New York). 'Having been thrown out of one tribe, they created their own new tribe,' Preston writes. 'While the new tribe offered an option richer than ever dreamed of before, it seldom allowed the gay man any compromise' (Preston, 1991, p. xii).

Sociologist James Jasper calls this the 'stigmatized identity' dilemma: an oppressed group wants to mobilize to fight stereotypes and to fit in, to appear respectable. But by doing so, by integrating within mainstream society, they undermine their own basis (and reason for existence), which is based on a distinctive identity. Paradoxically, it is hard to maintain the latter without some oppression from the mainstream, often in the form of legal discrimination (see also Duyvendak and Nederland, 2006; Jasper, 2006).

Although the Castro subculture witnessed much *collective* identity-building, subtle forms of identity specialization occurred as well. This coding and symbolic play often took place in relation to the most contested aspects of gay experience: the body and sexuality. Gay men developed their own sexual codes, dress preferences and norms regarding physical appearance, thereby distinguishing themselves to the outside world and creating a familiar, recognizable 'we'. And while these codes developed in neighborhoods like the Castro, they rapidly spread all over the (Western) world (Chabot and Duyvendak, 2002). The diffusion of these codes facilitated the growth of international solidarity, sustaining the idea of being part of a worldwide movement (Adam *et al.*, 1999). The Castro shows how home-making practices in a very *particular* place facilitated the *worldwide* diffusion of an imaginary gay home. The Castro became a symbolic place, a symbolic home for gays and lesbians around the world (Howe, 2001). And as subcultural codes began to travel, the local sense of familiarity became detached from geography: processes of cultural diffusion allowed feeling at home with others far away instead of with those next door. In a sense, the worldwide imitation of the subcultural codes of the Castro – a *gay generic* style – made the San Francisco neighborhood a less unique and particular place.

Valuing communities

San Francisco policy-makers did not hinder the development of a gay neighborhood, not only out of respect for the housing market (in which the government is not expected to intervene) but also because the existence of place-bound communities affirmed the city govern-ment's desired image of 'a city of many neighborhoods' (Godfroy, 1988; Pamuk, 2004). Although homosexuals were not protected from harassment and persecution for many years (Beemyn, 1997, p. 87), gays and lesbians in San Francisco have, since the 1960s, become one among many 'ethnic minorities' (Gamson, 1995). During elections, territoriality plays an important role as council members elected by districts and neighborhoods favor residentially concentrated com-munities. When, in the 1970s, the Castro gained its first homosexual representative, the famous late Harvey Milk, gays and lesbians were able to fully enter politics to further their social emancipation. The gay community thus seized on an existing opening in the political system – district voting – to promote its interests and to protect its members, especially during the AIDS epidemic in the 1980s.

San Francisco's support of the Castro was further shown by the city's $100,000 grant towards a project to keep the area's gay iden-tity intact. The project was fueled by fears of the disintegration of this famous gay and lesbian neighborhood (Buchanan, 2007) due to the migration of straight couples into the Castro and the flight of gay couples to suburban (and less expensive) neighborhoods in the Bay Area. These developments reveal a blurring of lines between heterosexuals and homosexuals as well as less antagonistic rela-tions between the mainstream and marginal segments of society. Furthermore, the number of gays and lesbians living in the Mid-West who feel compelled to move to the big cities has declined sharply: while in 1990 same-sex couples had an average geographic mobility more than twice that of same-race heterosexual married couples, this is no longer the case (Rosenfeld and Byung-Soo, 2005, p. 552). The growing acceptance of homosexuality is, moreover, not limited to larger urban areas; gays and lesbians in rural areas benefit from this trend as well. Whereas in 1990 same-sex couples often lived in city centers, during the 1990s the number of non-traditional couples living in cities actually declined (*ibid.*, p. 554). Though research on this development is still in its infancy, we can assume that gays and lesbians can feel more at home in their hometowns than ever before.

Conclusion: the promises and pitfalls of communities

In both the cases discussed above, movement activists entertained high hopes for caring communities – particularly for the role they would play in the 'coming out' of their respective constituencies. The mentally handicapped and psychiatric patients would exit from institutions to live 'normal' lives among 'normal' people in welcoming communities; gays and lesbians would live according to their sexual preferences in places of their own choosing.

What actually happened was quite different. Though people with intellectual disabilities indeed left their 'total institutions', for many their place of arrival was not a warm, welcoming community. Depending on the circumstances, some ended up on the street (this occurred in many US cities). In welfare states such as the Netherlands, individuals received their own housing but did not meaningfully integrate within communities or society at large. 'Normal' communities proved to be far from receptive. Our research also revealed that the new arrivals were themselves often reluctant to integrate: their home-making practices focused on the creation of safe havens for themselves, not on 'heavenly' places to publicly live out their identities. This inward-orientation was in part a fear of social rejection; it also had to do with their handicaps and the sincere wish to be on their own in dealing with their special situation. In other words, the idea of 'normalization' in, by and through communities seems questionable.

The specific nature of communities revealed itself in the case of the Castro as well, where the creation of a public gay home came at the price of tendencies towards homogenization and exclusion. After establishing their own place, gays began to protect their homes from outside invaders, be they Starbucks, the cable car or straight families. Deviant (read: straight) newcomers were not welcome in the self-defined gay community, creating the uneasy situation where those who had been excluded for so long were now excluding others. It was argued that this was necessary to protect the area for gays and lesbians – not only for those who lived in the Castro, but for gays and lesbians around the world, for whom this particular San Francisco neighborhood had become a symbol for the right to have your own place, the right to belong.

Compared to the crisis of home at the *household* level in the US, the example of the Castro shows vibrant feelings of belonging at the *community* level. This, however, came at a price: to be a public, 'heavenly' home, the community had to be quite homogeneous. As we will see in the next chapter, communities thus understood pose even larger problems at the national level: communities defined in terms of a shared home inevitably produce insiders and outsiders.

What could the community level realistically contribute to ease the crisis of home-at-home in the US? While community organizations could play a role to better balance care and paid work (for example by providing childcare and other social services), the profound changes necessary to overcome the inability to feel-at-home-at-home – for example less traditional male gender roles – are not likely to be found in communities.

Few people will dispute other people's right to feel at home with fellow citizens who share their interests, affinities, longings, histories, hobbies, etc. Feeling at home as an exclusive and selective emotion is hardly a problem when home is lived as a 'haven' – in private. But living home-as-heaven – the public manifestation of home feelings by an exclusive group on a territory claimed as their own – can be much more problematic. The Castro in this sense is an interesting but extreme case: most neighborhoods where gays and lesbians live are far more mixed in terms of sexual preference. But it was precisely the Castro's homogeneous character that brought its inhabitants political power (particularly in an electoral system based on territorial entities). The Castro's representatives could pursue a politics of home that fit into the larger narrative of San Francisco as a 'city of communities', allowing gays and lesbians to connect to the broader political world in order to protect their interests. This was in sharp contrast to the other social movement analyzed in this chapter. Without a clear idea of what their new communal home would be, home for the mentally handicapped remained, at best, a haven.

5
Feeling at Home in the Nation? Understanding Dutch Nostalgia

Introduction

If we want to better understand the political and social crisis engulfing many West European countries, we have to examine the feelings of alienation among native-born citizens who claim to no longer feel at home in their 'own' country. Their alienation is invariably blamed on the increasing number of immigrants in their midst. Rightwing populist parties, on the rise in many countries, see the presence of immigrants as a threat to social cohesion and to 'their' national 'homes'. The cultural 'deviance' of immigrants is considered incompatible with being Dutch, Danish, British, French, German, etc.

The debate over 'the stolen home' is deeply nostalgic. The past is portrayed as a closed and conflict-free whole, carried by citizens who all basically shared the same beliefs, norms and traditions. On the basis of this closed conception of culture, the invective focuses on the actual or potential harmful influences of in particular minorities with Muslim backgrounds, who form the majority of the immigrant population in Western Europe.

This closed conception of culture is prominent in the Dutch debate and is embraced by many native Dutch, who increasingly tend to fear Islam (Duyvendak *et al.*, 2010; Entzinger and Dourleijn, 2008; EUMC, 2002; Scheepers *et al.*, 2002). The building of mosques, the call to prayer, the use of religious symbols such as the headscarf, gender inequality, anti-integration pronouncements by ultra-orthodox imams and Islam-inspired political extremism are all popular subjects in the media and are often portrayed as corroding

Dutch culture (e.g., Mepschen *et al.*, 2010; Uitermark *et al.*, 2005; Verhaar and Saharso, 2004). In the Netherlands, the Islamophobic List Pim Fortuyn (LPF) party came second in the 2002 elections. Since then, the idea that Islam is alien to Dutch culture has gained currency. The religion's visible manifestations – the 'Islamization of the Netherlands' – are definitely considered 'out of place' by the most vocal voices in the public and political debate (Uitermark, 2010).

While we saw in Chapter 3 that the uneven outcomes of the gender revolution is largely behind the crisis of home in the US, the crisis of home in Western Europe can be traced back to the mobility revolution of goods and, especially, people. Whereas the embattled home in the US is experienced most acutely at the level of households, in Western Europe the crisis is framed at the level of nations and their putatively lost homelands. The current chapter examines how a certain perception of immigration articulated in the political and public debate has fueled feelings of alienation among the native-born in the Netherlands. I first analyze the alleged causes of the crisis. Of particular interest here is the Dutch 'retreat from multiculturalism' since the Netherlands was supposedly one of its standard-bearers in Europe. In the second half of the chapter, I focus on the various meanings attached to 'home' in the public and political debate, especially those that frame the nation-as-home. I will show that the conceptualization of the nation as a 'private home' is particularly problematic: when 'haven' and 'heaven' are conflated, little room is left for minorities. Uitermark (*ibid.*) has recently argued that the prominence of 'culturalists' in the public debate does not equal the silencing of more pragmatist, less populist voices. While this may be true, his study also convincingly shows that those who frame the nation as home are leading the public and political debate.

A multicultural paradise?

What caused the social and political crisis around the 'integration' of immigrants in the Netherlands, a country often jealously described as an oasis of tolerance? According to Joppke (2004, p. 248), allowing designated minority groups to 'emancipate' themselves within their own parallel institutions fuelled segregation. Other scholars also claim that Dutch 'multiculturalist' policies had pernicious effects on the cultural (and economic) integration of immigrants (Ireland, 2004;

Koopmans, 2002; Koopmans and Statham, 2000; Koopmans *et al.*, 2005). Sniderman and Hagendoorn write: 'In the Netherlands, as much as can be done on behalf of multiculturalism has been done. ... It promoted the most ambitious program of multiculturalism in Western Europe. ... The politics of the Netherlands since the assassination of Fortuyn has been the politics of multiculturalism in extremis' (2006, pp. 15–20). In their view, radical multiculturalism caused enormous tensions in the Netherlands: 'The whole thrust of multiculturalism is to accentuate, even exaggerate, differences between majority and minority and insist on their importance. ... Sharing a common identity builds support for inclusion; bringing differences of ethnic and religious identity to the fore evokes the very exclusionary reactions it is meant to avoid' (*ibid.*, pp. 15, 135).

In the above perspective, *multiculturalist policies* created feelings of 'homelessness', estrangement and alienation among the native Dutch, who were taught to respect migrants as 'others' in their 'own' country. To understand the Dutch crisis of home, we first have to answer the question whether it was indeed multiculturalism that undermined feelings of home. Were Dutch policies really multiculturalist?

The entire idea of the Dutch being (radical) multiculturalists is an inaccurate picture of what really happened and happens in the Netherlands (Duyvendak *et al.*, 2009; Duyvendak and Scholten, 2009). Policies that focused on the socio-cultural position of immigrants were much more various than the accounts of, for instance, Sniderman and Hagendoorn suggest. The 1970s policy on cultural identity can easily be misunderstood as multiculturalist, for its central tenet was that 'guest workers' should maintain their identities. The reason for this, however, was not to accommodate pluralism in the Netherlands, but to facilitate guest workers' return after they had fulfilled their function as unskilled laborers in the Netherlands (Ghorashi, 2003). In the early 1980s, when it became clear that most migrants were going to stay, policies turned to the ideal of group empowerment as a means towards their 'emancipation'. While these policies initially built on the legacy of 'pillarization'[1] that characterized Dutch social structure well into the 1960s, the emphasis on group empowerment faded over the 1980s as the objectives of *individual* socio-economic integration and participation took center stage (Duyvendak and Scholten, 2009).

While Koopmans *et al.*, like Sniderman and Hagendoorn, label the Dutch situation 'culturally pluralist' – even increasingly pluralist (2005, p. 73) – this gives a misleading picture of what government policies were promoting. Tolerance for immigrants' religious practices had little to do with national integration policies, let alone radical multiculturalism. Migrants' use of group-specific provisions was made possible by the Dutch institutional framework of 'pillars'; to the extent that this provided a basis for creating migrant religious and cultural institutions, it had nothing to do with 'pluralist' integration policies (Duyvendak *et al.*, 2004; Rath *et al.*, 1999). Most politicians were reluctant to support the development of a new (Islamic) religious 'pillar'. From the 1970s onwards, local governments, in fact, tried to prohibit immigrants from claiming their rights as Dutch citizens to set up Muslim schools (Feirabend and Rath, 1996). What may have appeared as a multicultural model to the outside world was, in reality, an amalgamation of ever-changing measures formulated by pragmatist policy-makers with little enthusiasm for group policies (Bertossi and Duyvendak, 2009). The 'long 1960s' did not produce multiculturalism in the Netherlands, but a rather homogeneous progressive moral majority.

If the 'multicultural model' did not fuel the recent political and social polarization in the Netherlands, then what did? What makes politicians claim that the native Dutch feel less at home in their country? I argue that a culturalized notion of citizenship has come to dominate the Dutch debate on the integration of immigrants, in which the Dutch 'progressive' culture is increasingly depicted as a product of timeless consensus. To guard against harmful external influences, this culture has to be restored and protected. Immigrants have to prove their loyalty to it, prove that they feel at home in their country of settlement by subscribing to its dominant ideas, convictions, habits and emotions (Geschiere, 2009). If they don't, politicians claim, the native-born will no longer feel at home in their 'own' country.

The Dutch cultural consensus (and some dissensus)

Contrary to popular wisdom, the current crisis of home in the Netherlands is not the result of 'failed' multiculturalism. Over the past decades, Dutch policy-makers have not pursued full-fledged multiculturalist policies promoting the pluralist religious and cultural identities of all minority groups (Duyvendak and Scholten, 2009). They instead focused on socio-economically disadvantaged ethnic minorities (Uitermark, 2010). While the tradition of pillarization gave leeway to some Islamic institutions, integration policies never straightforwardly promoted immigrant cultural and/or religious identities.

Another, related, misunderstanding is that the Netherlands has developed into a pluralist, highly diverse society. In fact, since the 1970s, the majority population has rapidly become more culturally homogeneous. Whereas in many countries, including the US, majority opinion is divided on issues of gender, family and sexuality, almost the entire political spectrum of the Dutch majority population supports progressive values on these matters. After a period of intense cultural polarization during the 'long 1960s', the majority has developed rather uniform, progressive ideals according to the Euro-barometer, European Social Survey, European Values Study, International Social Survey Program and the Continuous Tracking Survey (as recapitulated in Arts *et al.*, 2003; Duyvendak *et al.*, 2004; Halman *et al.*, 2005; Jansen, 2008; SCP, 1998; Uitterhoeve, 2000). More than anywhere else, the majority population in the Netherlands believes that divorce is acceptable and homosexuality nothing out of the ordinary. More than most other Europeans (let alone Americans), the Dutch disagree with conservative propositions such as 'women must have children to be happy', 'a child should respect its parents', or 'we would be better off were we to return to a traditional way of life'; the Dutch are among the most ardent supporters of secular, nontraditional values and rights to freedom of speech and expression (Inglehart and Baker, 2000; Inglehart and Welzel, 2005). Differences in values between more and less highly educated people, moreover, are slight; the Netherlands is now among the three least culturally polarized countries in Europe (Achterberg, 2006, p. 55).

As traditional values around family, marriage and sexuality lost ground, the Netherlands became less preoccupied with the Christian tradition – and vice versa (de Koster *et al.*, 2010). Figure 5.1 (Houtman *et al.*, 2008) shows that polarization over these values has declined since 1970 (increasing standard deviations point to growing differences of understanding and cultural polarization; decreasing standard deviations point to growing agreement; for authoritarianism see below).[2]

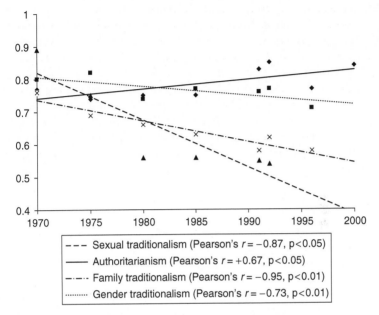

Figure 5.1 Diverging patterns for moral traditionalism and authoritarianism (1970–2000)

Source: Houtman *et al.* 2008.

This decline in cultural polarization was largely due to the new progressive moral consensus that distanced itself from moral (i.e., sexual, family and gender) traditionalism (Duyvendak, 2004; Houtman and Duyvendak, 2009).

The increasing polarization around authoritarianism

The Dutch majority tends to demand that migrants share their 'modern' and 'progressive' values. This in part reflects the strength of the consensus within the majority population. In this respect, the Netherlands is similar to Denmark, which also has a clearly 'enlightened' moral majority. It may come as a surprise that a progressive and 'tolerant' country demands conformity from those whose views are not progressive. When it comes to values, liberal countries evidently need not esteem diversity in opinions (e.g., Lægaard, 2007; Wikan, 2002). The cultural consensus among the Dutch goes hand in hand with the dismissal of other values. As Buruma has observed: 'Tolerance, then, has its limits even for Dutch progressives. It is easy to be tolerant of those who are much like us. ... It is much harder to extend the same principle to the strangers in our midst, who find our ways as disturbing as we do theirs' (2006, p. 128). Pillarization may once have accommodated pluralism in the Netherlands. But pluralism today is a weak shadow; the growing consensus around progressive values has created a wider values gap between the native majority and Muslim immigrants than in countries with less progressive majority cultures. As Van der Veer puts it:

> For the Dutch, Muslims stand for theft of enjoyment. Their strict sexual morals remind the Dutch too much of what they have so recently left behind ... In a society where consumption and especially the public performance of sexual identity have become so important, the strict clothing habits of observant Muslims are an eyesore. (2006, pp. 119–20)

However, survey results show increasing support for so-called 'Western values' among immigrants and their offspring; proportionately more immigrants in the Netherlands have come to share this progressive culture than anywhere else (Dagevos *et al.*, 2003; Dagevos *et al.*, 2007; Entzinger and Dourleijn, 2008). This progressive cultural consensus has also provided opportunities for (ex)Muslims – including famous ex-politician Hirsi Ali, who fervently objected to sexism in the Koran – to protest against sexism, homophobia and the lack of freedom of speech within Islamic texts and Muslim traditions (Mepschen *et al.*, 2010). On the other hand, the values gap between Muslim groups and the majority population is wider in the Netherlands than in most other countries. It is wider than in Germany on issues such as adherence to community and conservative values (Demant, 2005).

All in all, it is clear that the Dutch majority population increasingly sees cultural differences as a problem (Entzinger and Dourleijn, 2008). In the political debate, populist and rightwing parties reveal their allergy to cultural differences and believe immigrants should be forced to assimilate or 'go home'.

Hence the advancement of progressive values – embraced now by both the political Left and Right – goes hand in hand with the belief, trumpeted by vocal politicians, that everyone has to adhere to them. Debate in Dutch politics no longer focuses on *substantial* topics; it is the *procedural* question of how to deal with those who don't share 'modern' values that polarizes the political spectrum as nothing else. So whereas cultural polarization on moral traditionalism has declined since 1970, polarization on authoritarianism (defending the social order, ethnocentrism, how to deal with cultural differences) has grown (compare de Koster and van der Waal, 2006) (see Figures 5.1 and 5.2, both based on Houtman *et al.*, 2008).

This is also apparent in the programs of Dutch political parties over the period 1950–98. Figure 5.2 shows that over this period, polarization over moral traditionalism (regarding all sorts of moral issues) declined, while polarization over authoritarianism (how to deal with those who buck the consensus) grew. Figure 5.2 is based on so-called Party Manifesto Data (Budge *et al.*, 2001), which quantifies

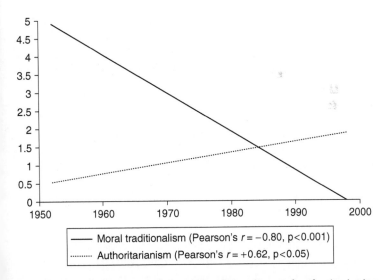

Figure 5.2 Diverging patterns for moral traditionalism and authoritarianism in Dutch political party programs (fourteen elections years between 1950 and 1998)

Source: Houtman *et al.* 2008.

the attention political party programs give to a comprehensive list of policy priorities (for analysis of this data see Achterberg, 2006).[3] The data make it clear that the decline of support for traditional moral values has fueled a new cultural polarization over the importance of individual freedom and cultural pluralism. Among the supporters of authoritarianism we see the desire for uniformity and community, and preference for ethnocentrism and a shared 'home'. Deviation from dominant norms and values – even though these values have become unabashedly liberal – is not tolerated. Liberal values have become national values: 'If it is possible for social actors to present liberal values in public discourse in a way that makes them the symbolic basis for a socially effective distinction between "us" (the nation) and "others", then the characterization of the values as national values makes sense' (Lægaard, 2007, p. 45).

The culturalization of citizenship

The rise of authoritarianism has fueled the culturalization of citizenship: a process in which emotions, feelings, norms and values, symbols and traditions (including religion) come to play a pivotal role in defining what can be expected of a Dutch citizen.

While its recent manifestations are unique, the culturalization of citizenship is not a new phenomenon. Citizenship has long been defined by the nation's dominant culture and ethnic group. Nevertheless, the idea of *national* and *mono-cultural* citizenship has been questioned over the past decades. First, it became increasingly difficult to conceive of national citizenship as strictly mono-cultural because citizens of the same country have increasingly diverse cultural and ethnic backgrounds: their roots are *transnational* while their loyalties and feelings of belonging are often pluri-national. Second, as has been argued in the communitarian tradition, citizenship is more often experienced at the *local* rather than national level (Sandel, 1982; Walzer, 1983).

It is in the context of these 'glocalizing' tendencies that the culturalization of *national* citizenship is taking place. Here the 'native' culture is seen as under threat, leading to the normative project of defining and protecting 'traditional' cultural heritage (for instance, in the form of a 'canon' and teaching it to newcomers in citizenship courses). This process underscores the *emotional* aspects of citizenship, which has evolved from a status or practice into a deep sentiment. Citizens are subjected to new 'feeling rules' (Hochschild, 2003, p. 82). Belonging – feeling at home – has become a requirement (Morley, 2001). Particularly at the national level, new 'feeling rules' are applied to immigrants who are increasingly expected to demonstrate feelings of attachment, belonging, connectedness and loyalty to their new country. Because feelings as such cannot easily be perceived, certain actions become their symbolic stand-ins (Verkaaik, 2010). For example, having dual nationality has come to represent lack of loyalty to Dutch culture in the eyes of a majority of Dutch politicians.

Emotive culturalization thus stresses the need for loyalty to the nation-state and demands proof of such feelings from immigrants. It includes the warning that immigrants who do not manage to feel at home should go 'home' – that is, disappear altogether from their 'country of arrival' – even when they are born and raised in the Netherlands (Duyvendak, 2007). To quote Jan Marijnissen, at the time the Chairman of the leftwing Socialist Party:

> The Muslim community must understand that there is a collective responsibility to combat excesses such as political Islam. Educators, teachers and imams must choose for our Constitution and bring up children in its spirit. If one is not prepared to conform to our values and obey our laws, the pressing advice is: seek a country where you feel at home. (Marijnissen, 2004)

If immigrants want to stay in the Netherlands, they have to adapt to 'Dutch' norms, values and emotions. 'The idea seems to be, indeed, that Dutch identity must "cannibalize" other identities in order to turn immigrants into reliable citizens' (Geschiere, 2009, p. 166).

The Marijnissen quote shows that the culturalization of citizenship has a different but equally heavy influence on both leftwing and rightwing political parties. While the latter were pushed to embrace 'substantial' progressive values – an overall move of the political spectrum towards the left – the leftwing parties became far less tolerant towards immigrants who allegedly did not conform to Dutch 'norms and values'. Marijnissen literally frames the 'solution' for the assumed 'non-fit' between immigrants (with Muslim backgrounds) and 'the Dutch' in terms of another home: 'Seek a country where you feel at home'. What does this imply? Immigrants report in surveys that they do feel at home in the Netherlands (see below); what is lacking – in Marijnissen's view – are the deep feelings of attachment and loyalty to the Netherlands on the basis of a fit between one's personal norms and values and those of the country. In other words, Marijnissen assumes that a normative and cognitive fit regarding values is a precondition for truly feeling at home: immigrants have to share in his rather uniform public 'heaven' conception of home. That immigrants report feeling at home in the Netherlands while allegedly disagreeing with (some of) its dominant norms and values implies their adherence to a more private, haven-like conception of home – a type of home unacceptable to the leader of the Socialist Party.

(Not) feeling at home in the Netherlands

Most of the elements that ignite the debate in the Netherlands – and in other West European countries – can be traced to the emotionalization of what it means to be a citizen. In debates over dual citizenship, spokespersons of various political parties emphasize that citizenship is more than a 'formality': 'To have Dutch nationality is more than having a Dutch passport. It is an expression of feeling at home in Dutch society, in her democratic legal order, her values, norms and mentality. You must, in other words, fully focus on Dutch society' (Jacques Niederer (VVD), in Dutch Parliament [Tweede Kamer], 2000a, p. 3640). 'People must feel connected to our society if they want to be naturalized, they have to feel at home in it. It is necessary to feel Dutch' (Maxime Verhagen (CDA), in Dutch Parliament [Tweede Kamer], 2000a, p. 3635). Politicians thus tell immigrants how to *feel* – above all, to *feel at home* in the Netherlands.

But as we will see, many immigrants claim that they already feel at home in the Netherlands – data show that some immigrant groups even feel more at home than the native Dutch (see Table 5.1 on p. 102). Why, then, this strong and widely held suspicion that immigrants don't feel at home in the country? For some Dutch politicians, it may simply be unimaginable that (Muslim) immigrants can feel at home in the Netherlands. Others don't accept the manner in which immigrants feel at home: they see an enormous gap with how they think a 'real' Dutch citizen should behave, dress, think and feel. A veiled woman simply cannot feel Dutch, or at home in a country that – at least discursively – embraces gender equality.

This assumed incompatibility between 'us' and 'them' not only fuels suspicions that immigrants don't really feel at home in the Netherlands; the corollary is the claim that the native Dutch feel less at home as well: they cannot imagine sharing their 'home' with people who have such alien norms and values (de Gruijter *et al.*, 2010). Hence on the basis of a certain conception of 'home' – everybody shares the same norms, values, practices, habits – Muslim immigrants are suspected of disloyalty. Or even worse, of terrorism. As the former leader of the Labor Party Wouter Bos put it recently: 'Take the ordinary, law-abiding citizen faced with the arrival of terrorism from other countries and cultures, who wonders why terrorists call themselves true Muslims and what this says about the next-door neighbor, who happens to be a Muslim too' (Bos, 2008, p. 2).

My analysis of parliamentary debates shows that, over time, the crisis in 'feeling at home' has indeed become primarily a problem for the native-born. In the 1990s, and around 2000, 'not feeling at home' was still mostly discussed as a problem for immigrants, which Dutch society should help overcome – for instance by adding 'sending country' elements to Dutch architecture (Lucy Kortram (PvdA), in Dutch Parliament [Tweede Kamer], 2000b, p. 882). After 2002 (the murder of Pim Fortuyn), and even more after 2004 (the murder of Theo van Gogh, see Buruma, 2006), discussions about the loss of home feelings have almost invariably concerned the native Dutch, whom politicians increasingly paint as 'foreigners' in their own country, cities and neighborhoods.

The alleged 'homelessness' of the native Dutch

A recent official government report gives the following reason why native Dutch today would feel less at home:

> Feelings about what is 'normal' and self-evident determine whether or not people feel at home or accepted in their environment. For this reason alone, the influx of immigrants – in the district, the school, the association, the working environment – go hand in hand with

feelings of unease, loss and even insecurity. These feelings become stronger as the behavior of newcomers more strongly deviates from what is considered normal, especially in the case of criminal or other beyond-the-pale behavior. (Dutch Cabinet, 2008, p. 6)

In response to reproaches that it has long overlooked the interests and feelings of its working-class constituency, the Dutch Labor Party has recently begun paying great attention to how immigration has undermined 'feeling at home' among the native-born. I present here three rather long quotes from spokespersons of this party to illustrate the pivotal role of feelings of alienation within Dutch politics. In the first quote, the leader of the party in parliament in 2007 reflects upon developments in disadvantaged neighborhoods. Jacques Tichelaar:

> The PvdA is very aware that it is always the people with the lowest incomes living in disadvantaged neighborhoods who are the first to be confronted with the coming of foreigners. On top of their own problems, they are now saddled with the problems that the newcomers bring with them. We ask much of the inhabitants of these areas.... We have great admiration for them, their forbearance, their support for newcomers and their contribution to a better Netherlands and we understand that sometimes it is also just too much. (Dutch Parliament, 2007, p. 2666).

His sympathy is all for the native-born who are 'fed up' with the (problems allegedly caused by) 'foreigners' (a rather a-typical word in the Dutch debate, out of use since the late 1970s as it 'others' immigrants, including those born and raised in the Netherlands and/or those who have Dutch nationality). It shows that the Labor Party shares in the dominant framing of the issue: a minority of 'aliens' has caused the majority's feelings of alienation.

The second quote expresses the idea that it is patently unjust that those who have been 'rooted' in the Netherlands for generations are now suffering from such feelings of alienation. As it reads in a recent Labor Party white paper on migration and integration:

> These feelings of loss and uneasiness we also know in the Netherlands. Not only among residents of working class city

districts, but broadly in society. Neighborhoods built for workers and the middle class have become migrant districts. Well-known social customs have disappeared. Shared codes of conduct are no longer self-evident. The continuous influx of new residents requires a great deal from the residents, as well as from the school, the general practitioner and the district agent. But also in places in our country where apparently nothing has changed, people have experienced feelings of unease. Their country is changing and they feel alienated. They feel that the changes have been foisted upon them – and that is a nasty feeling when it comes to the country where you were born and raised, which you, your parents and their parents built up. (PvdA, 2009)

The native Dutch, it is implied in the above quote, have more rights to the neighborhood since they were born and raised there – a rather odd argument since the same is true for all second-generation immigrants. Note also that teachers, general practitioners and district agents seem, almost by definition, to be native-born Dutch. But more significant is the idea of 'home' underlying this thinking: people can only feel at home with those who have been part of that home for a long time and who share the same norms and values.

In the third quote, the 'foreigners' turn out to be Muslims: cultural and religious elements are interwoven in the discourse opposing Muslims and Dutch society. As the leader of the Labor Party in parliament, Mariëtte Hamer, put it in 2008:

Integration causes pain. Pain for the native who feels that his neighborhood has been taken over by foreigners. Pain for the Turk who has done his best to build up a life in the Netherlands, but is blocked by a lot of incomprehension. And yes, also pain for the countryside resident who has never seen a foreigner in his town, but truly feels that the Netherlands is no longer as it was. Dutch society has taken in large groups of foreigners over the past decades. For a large number of Dutchmen, confrontation with other cultures, customs and beliefs is an uncomfortable everyday reality. I have experienced at close hand how drastic this can be. My mother saw her district...change dramatically within 20 years. What was once the hopeful new Amsterdam has degenerated into a district where one no longer feels at home. Concerns over changes in society are reinforced by radical Muslims committing terrorist acts in the name of Islam. Fatwas have been proclaimed. On the Linnaeusstraat in Amsterdam East, Theo van Gogh was murdered in a horrible manner. This was all directed against our open, Western society, against everything we stand for. (Dutch Parliament [Tweede Kamer], 2008a, p. 4884).

The discourse is constructed in such a way that an opposition develops between 'we' (native-born, modern, Western, not feeling at home anymore) and 'them' (coming from a different 'culture', of whom the most radical randomly kill). The obvious intention here is to take the feelings of the native Dutch ('my mother') seriously: 'we' empathize with those who no longer feel at home in what was once their hopeful neighborhood and country. The native Dutch, it is argued, have become like foreigners in their own country, feeling what foreigners should allegedly feel: not at home. But as many 'foreigners' now report that they *do* feel at home, the world for the native-born has truly been turned upside down: foreigners are experiencing feelings that should belong to the native-born while the native-born feel like foreigners. Politicians suggest that the native Dutch feel estranged and besieged by immigrants, and are therefore in a legitimate position 'to claim their country back'.

There is a way to 'reclaim the country'. This is to (further) develop a 'thick' notion of what it is to be Dutch. This will make it impossible for foreigners to claim 'Dutchness' and/or to feel at home since they can't know their new home, its history, traditions, customs and feelings as well as the native-born (allegedly) do. Foreigners aren't part of this history; they have no roots here. By embracing the 'roots paradigm', feeling at home is denied to immigrants. 'Being rooted' not only ensures knowledge of what it is to be authentically Dutch but the historical right to define what that is as well. Let's see how this works.

A thick notion of 'home'

Dutch politicians from both the Left and Right plead for new forms of 'nationalism' and 'patriotism', claiming that the Dutch to date have had a very 'thin' notion of national identity. Another quote from the former leader of the leftwing Socialist Party, Jan Marijnissen, is illustrative:

In the Netherlands we have not sufficiently appreciated our own history and what gives us the feeling of being at home. It has to do with the making of the physical environment, but also the cultural and moral environment. And also parliamentary democracy, all that gives us the feeling: 'we are at home here'. ... My argument is ... that our view of the world has a lot to do with the land on which we stand. And that land on which we stand is what I would call the *Heimat* (I borrow it from the Germans because it is such a fine word). But also to indicate that it is not only ... the physical home, it is the knowledge that if you send your child to school he will get a good education. (2008)

Who is 'us' in these passages? 'Us' identifies with the 'soil': to feel at home is to be rooted, a quality apparently more common among the native-born than among immigrants. But not only the soil: moral, cultural, social and educational aspects of life are all part of what makes the Netherlands home for 'us'. Taken together, it implies a very thick notion of what is necessary to feel at home in the Netherlands.

Mobilizing a thick notion of home runs the risk that instead of including (what might have been Marijnissen's intention), one excludes those who don't (want to) share this notion of home. Such exclusion is already taking place as the Dutch have a much thicker national identity than most of them are aware of. As Halle Ghorashi concludes on the basis of her research on exiled Iranian women in the US and the Netherlands:

In contradiction to the United States, the Dutch notion of national identity is exclusive and thick. By the thickness of national identity, I mean that there is a common understanding of Dutchness based on color, 'roots', and certain codes of behavior that excludes difference. These codes of behavior are in many ways related to a Calvinist background with expectations expressing certain behavior. This thick notion of national identity leads to a process of exclusion and sets up a dichotomous relationship between us and them. ... The consequence is that people from different backgrounds who are born in the Netherlands, or who have lived most of their lives there and have Dutch nationality are not included as 'one of us'. (2003, p. 255)

Knowledge of this historically rooted national identity – though presented as something to aid immigrants' integration – on balance works as a balm for those 'dispossessed' native Dutch who hope to regain their former position. The historicization of citizenship favors those who have 'always' been here: not due to any cognitive considerations (since everybody can learn Dutch history), but due to its 'ontological' implications: native Dutch are indisputably part of it all, whereas immigrants are by definition not part of this specific history. The native position is not in question, along with their views on what is required to feel at home in the Netherlands. The following quote from the spokesman of the small conservative Christian party illustrates the demand for unconditional emotional investment in the new country. It implies that only one conception of feeling at home is acceptable for immigrants: warm feelings for the 'home country' (a more private, haven-like conception of home is out of the question):

> In order to express loyalty to the Netherlands, the ChristenUnie (CU) party is in favor of prospective Dutchmen, at the time of naturalization, to make explicitly clear their inner commitment to their new 'home' country. It could take the form of a declaration of loyalty. In any case, an explicit proclamation of loyalty to the Dutch society of which the newcomer is now a permanent part is crucial. (Tineke Huizinga-Heringa (CU) in: Dutch Parliament [Tweede Kamer], 2004)

The majority thus uses its power of definition to proclaim how things are done (or are allowed and tolerated) in the Netherlands, while recent proposals to establish historical canons and a national historic museum are further examples of attempts to define the nation's character. All of this is justified by the idea, expressed by among others the publicist Paul Scheffer (2007), that newcomers will only be able to 'feel at home' when 'the Dutch' can more clearly formulate where 'we' stand. So that 'they' will be able to comprehend, 'we' – the natives – must define who 'we' are. At first sight, this may appear as acceptance of responsibility by the dominant group: only when 'we' clarify who we are, can 'they' be held accountable for their (un)willingness to integrate.

But are the politicians of the progressive majority failing to define what it stands for? No, there is little evidence of immigrants left in the dark by a country unwilling to reveal itself. Instead, we witness a dominant narrative that tells immigrants – and in particular those with Muslim backgrounds – that how they lead their lives is improper and maladapted, and that they therefore spoil the home feelings of the natives. The Netherlands has shown quite clearly what it stands for over these past years. The native Dutch identity has hardened, with paradoxical consequences. On the one hand, migrants are forced to identify with the Dutch nation more then ever before (other loyalties are not permitted, as feeling at home means feeling at home in the nation). On the other hand, the thickening and historical rooting of Dutch identity makes it much harder for newcomers to identify with.

In other words, the marginalization of immigrants has only been exacerbated by the historical roots attached to Dutch 'cultural' identity in recent years. Creating a canon more likely hinders than promotes citizenship. To begin with, familiarity with a canonical national past is poor preparation for citizenship in current society. Canonizing not only makes a mockery of the past; it ignores the malleability of the present. If the ticket into Dutch society can only be obtained by being part of a longer national history, people with different backgrounds are confronted with insurmountable obstacles. Dutch society then only becomes accessible to people with deep roots in Dutch soil. Citizenship is reduced to a property one has by birth, one that is unchanged through agency. What one does, what one contributes, one's readiness to become a part of the society in which one lives then no longer matter: immigrants (originally) come from elsewhere, have not experienced 'our' history and will therefore never really be 'one of us'.

The thick, historically rooted idea of 'home' thus has highly ambivalent and paradoxical effects. Though presented to 'support' immigrants, in reality it blocks their integration; obliged to feel at home in their country of residence, this 'home' is constructed in such a way that they can never really feel a part of it. Even when policy-makers wish to be inclusive, they seem to believe historical 'rooting' is the best way to stimulate belonging. The City of Amsterdam, for example, claims that 'too many residents ... do not identify with the city and do not know its history'. Under the slogan 'A Shared Vision of History and the Future', the aim of policy is for 'all residents of Amsterdam to feel themselves Amsterdammers: the number of residents who feel at home in Amsterdam should grow annually'. The way to attain such identification, the City Hall claims, is to teach residents about the city's history (City of Amsterdam, 2006).

Local and national politicians not only consider it their job to influence the deep feelings of belonging among their citizenry; they also claim to know what actually determines feeling at home and what role history plays in it. But is this true? This question is pertinent since data show (see below) that most immigrants feel quite at home in the Netherlands, and even more so at the local level. This, again, shows that policy-makers' assumptions about immigrants not feeling at home in the Netherlands don't hold. The alleged nexus between feeling at home and historical knowledge thus becomes even more questionable: since most immigrants claim that they feel at home in the country, this either implies that they are well versed in the history of the Netherlands or that historical knowledge is not a necessary condition for developing such feelings (which seems to me the more plausible case).

Since promoting a sense of belonging in the Netherlands is an official policy goal – 'The goal must be a society where everybody can feel at home' (Dutch Cabinet, 2008)[4] – it should come as no surprise that data on 'feeling at home' are collected by the main governmental social science research institute. These data show some correlation between juridical (citizenship) status and 'feeling at home'. But the most striking finding is the overall picture: around 70 percent of all immigrants feel at home in the Netherlands.

Table 5.1 Feeling at home in the Netherlands, by citizenship status and ethnic group (%)

	Turks	Moroccans
Dual nationality	68	74
Dutch nationality	78	80
Nationality of land of origin	61	51

Source: Advisory Committee for Refugee Affairs (2008)

As Chapters 1 and 2 revealed many possible meanings of 'feeling at home', the question is what these data tell us. We have to ask this as well since, in the qualitative research we carried out, most immigrants did not spontaneously express strong emotions regarding the Netherlands. Their responses suggested that there was not much for them to gain by identifying with the country, that it was difficult to relate their daily lives to a structure that has relatively little emotional meaning to them. Responses were generally of three kinds: that the issue was not of great concern; that it was not necessary to belong to only one country; and questioning the meaning of nationality itself. All avoided entering into deeper discussions about Dutch identity (Tonkens *et al.*, forthcoming).

Though the data show that this does not imply immigrants don't feel at home, their affirmation of belonging may be a response to their loyalty constantly being questioned. Recent research among Moroccans residing in different Western European countries seems to corroborate this interpretation. Dutch-Moroccans stand out for feeling at home in their country of residence; they are also highly aware of the negative labeling within the Dutch public and political debate (NRC correspondent, 2010). Hence exactly what their affirmation entails is an interesting question. In my understanding – given the various meanings of feeling at home, and in light of our qualitative data – Dutch-Moroccan home feelings do not seem to be connected to the *nation*. They know that Dutch politicians expect them to feel at home. But since the Dutch nation has exclusive connotations, they attach their home feelings to other objects, territories and people. Moreover, their notion of feeling at home may further shrink towards that of a safe haven since the culturalization of citizenship does not make it any easier for immigrants to feel a part of Dutch society. As Peter Geschiere points out: 'The central question raised by the Dutch experience, and by developments elsewhere in Europe, is whether giving greater substance to the national culture … makes integration of migrants easier. In practice, this seems rather to work toward a deepening of the divide and make integration all the more difficult' (Geschiere, 2009, p. 167).

In this deepening of the divide, some native-born are losers as well – losers in terms of not feeling at home, even though they blame others for not sufficiently belonging to the Netherlands.

America, the homeland?

The enormous popularity of the term 'homeland' in the US after 9/11 is, in fact, quite surprising; before then, the term was rarely heard. ' "Home" has a narrower meaning in American English than in British English. In Britain, the "home secretary", for example, attends to domestic (as distinct form foreign) affairs, and "home counties" means those shires bordering London. The American word "home", however, has as its primary meaning the house in which one lives' (Collins, 2007, p. 1). Collins explains that the new term 'homeland' could nonetheless resonate among (parts of the) American public because its protagonists – a coalition of secular conservatives and the religious Right – made strategic use of well-known biblical narratives. The idea of the US as 'God's own nation', the continuous use of the phrase 'God bless America', and the popular idea that Americans are 'chosen' all feed into the idea that this is a very special country, home to a very special people.

The rise of 'homeland' discourse has had an exclusionary effect on some immigrant groups, in particular Muslims immediately after 9/11. As for the situation of migrants more generally, homeland discourse seems to have had a permanent impact on those who want to enter the country. The moral panic is fueled by the (perceived) situation at the American–Mexican border. In public debate, Mexican migrants without papers are labeled illegal 'aliens' – a term that comes close to the imaginary surrounding migrants with Muslim backgrounds in Europe.

But for those migrants who are legally in, the situation seems to be back to normal. In the US – one of the most religious countries in the world – it is unimaginable to attack Muslims because of their religion in the way this is happening in some Western European countries, in particular those which are highly secularized such as Denmark and the Netherlands.

In the wake of 9/11, discourse in Western European countries turned to the need for greater social cohesion and patriotism (also because the perpetrators of 9/11 and the London and Madrid attacks were 'home-grown' Muslim Europeans). Many political leaders in Europe looked jealously to the US: 9/11 had united that country in patriotism. But public opinion in Europe misunderstood (and still misunderstands) the nature of this American nationalism – what I would term 'nationalism light'. Under the general heading of American citizenship, diversity is still very much welcomed. A rather 'thin' notion of national identity thus continues to prevail in the US,

> in which there is room for thick particularities. American national discourse allows thick cultural differences within its understanding of a thin notion of national identity. It is possible to be considered American – both by oneself as well as by others – within the diversity of physical appearances, languages, and cultural backgrounds. Thus, the notion of American identity is like an umbrella that includes different particularities. (Ghorashi, 2003, pp. 221–2)

Nevertheless, 9/11 had an impact since citizens – and in particular new immigrants – were expected to demonstrate loyalty to the nation, while the introduction of a Department of Homeland Security strengthened the idea of the nation as a 'home'. All this does not imply, however, that the transformations described for Europe above (as witnessed in the Netherlands) took place in the US as well, where the culturalization of citizenship remains rather weak.

Compared to Europe, the 'crisis of home' in the US is less acute at the *national* level, though some politicians mobilize feelings of insecurity and fear that 'overwhelm proactive aspects of home as a friendly place where residents feel safe and comfortable' (Low 2004, pp. 7–8). Here we can add that the post-9/11 moral panic concerning the vulnerable 'homeland' has only increased the sense of crisis at the household level: home as a 'safe haven' – one of the two fundamental meanings of home as we saw in Chapter 2 – is perhaps not so safe after all.

6

Conclusion: Inclusive Ways of Feeling at Home?

Introduction

As I have argued in this book – and many others have shown in their work – we need to take emotions related to 'feeling at home' very seriously. 'Belonging' is an existential need – even for the most chronically mobile among us (Gustafson, 2009; Nowicka, 2007). And while 'home-making' strategies may differ, 'home' is meaningful to everyone in one way or another. Being threatened in one's home feelings is one of the main reasons for all kinds of struggle and violence (Stein, 2001). As the vast literature on nationalism (Appadurai, 1990; Calhoun, 1999; Hearn, 2007; Holy, 1998; Scheff, 2006) shows, (the lack of) home feelings has been crucial for both those who want to create a 'pure' homeland and for those excluded from the nation, wandering in diaspora and longing to return (Abdelhandy, 2008; Marshall-Fratani, 2006; Rose, 2005; Thiranagama, 2007).

While feeling at home is an important emotion for all, it is at the same time a discriminating phenomenon: nobody feels at home everywhere and with everybody. The cosmopolitan dream thus ignores the sociological reality that feeling at home is a differentiating emotion: it necessarily divides those with whom we feel at home from the rest. If home is everywhere and we feel at home with everyone, 'home' tends to lose its meaning.

This book therefore examined where and when people (do not) feel at home and with what inclusionary or exclusionary effects. As it turned out, we have to distinguish between feeling at home in the private and public spheres. The crisis of home in the US – mostly experienced at the level of individual households – is of a different character than the 'national' crisis of home in Western European countries. This divergence also reveals itself in the two types of nostalgia it produces. Below, I discuss these two types of nostalgia as they relate to their respective crises of home. I then proceed to discuss two other spheres that proved to be important for home feelings: the workplace and the community. Comparing these four spheres will help to better grasp the various forms of belonging, particularly their differences in terms of inclusion and exclusion.

Two types of nostalgia: reflective and restorative

Our days are full of nostalgia. Even the discourse of the current president of the United States about *change* is not unequivocally future-oriented. Far from it: Barack Obama's speeches are often about restoring peace at home and rebuilding harmonious relationships within neighborhoods. Nostalgia is not necessarily problematic, so long as we understand that nostalgia says more about contemporary society than it does about the past (see Coontz's *The Way We Never Were*, 1992). Here, I will examine two different types of nostalgia as they prevail in the US and Western Europe, the societal and political cleavages that produce them, and their inclusionary and exclusionary effects. As it turns out, *not* feeling at home has far more pernicious effects in Western Europe than in the US. The revanchist version of nostalgia dominant in the old world has a strong exclusionary dynamic, whereas the more constructive nostalgia we see in the US has the potential to include all.

Both the gender revolution and globalization have transformed the world we live in. Women are no longer cloistered within home and hearth; their world has expanded enormously from working outside the house. Planned and unplanned migration have likewise changed the world, for migrants and receiving societies alike. Even if only 3 percent of the world's population is living outside their country of birth, intra-national mobility for many people has increased significantly while goods and images now circulate at an ever-faster rate (Urry, 2010). We can broadly understand these changes as an *enlargement* of the world: of more people identifying with more people in more places, and changing places more often.

It is noteworthy, though, that these *spatial* transformations have largely been interpreted as *temporal* developments. This is the case among social scientists, who witness modern societies transforming into postmodern ones, and within public and political debates more generally, where there is a fixation on identifying who is 'progressive' and who is 'backward'. Paradoxically, the Dutch belief in their own progressiveness goes together with an unprecedentedly strong desire to hang on to the past. The revolutions of our time have not made us more forward-looking, but more nostalgic. History is popular as never before; nostalgia for the *Heimat* is widespread. Home is no longer what it was: not for individuals (due to the uneven outcomes of the gender revolution) or for neighborhoods, let alone for nations (due to problems linked to migration and globalization). Politicians, furthermore, feed the nostalgic perspective. Many politicians – and not just the populists – feel that we can only address 'our uprootedness' by looking to the past.

In *The Future of Nostalgia* (2001), Svetlana Boym distinguishes between 'restorative' and 'reflective' nostalgia. Restorative nostalgia is a seemingly desperate longing for former times when things were allegedly real, original and authentic. Reflective nostalgia reflects upon the value of the (remembered) past for present purposes. For the former, the past must be reconquered at the cost of the present; for the latter, the question is how (more) continuity can be created between the past and present. When we compare nostalgia in the Netherlands and the US, the Dutch version seems primarily restorative, while in America nostalgia tends more towards the reflective form. Both, however, focus on loss: loss of the familiar nation in the Netherlands, loss of the familiar nuclear household in America. *Familiarity*, as we saw in Chapter 2, forms the basis of 'feeling at home'; it is a necessary aspect (but no guarantee) of it. But in both the Netherlands and the US today, the family (etymologically related to familiarity) can no longer be taken for granted. American family life is imploding under time pressure, while the Netherlands no longer feels itself to be a single national family. A feeling that a familiar home has been lost is widely felt in both countries.

But here the similarities stop and the differences begin. Home in the US is primarily a protected, private place (home-as-haven), whereas in the Netherlands the nation as a whole is seen as home, a public space where shared 'modern' conceptions concerning the 'good life' are nourished (home-as-heaven). The crisis of home in the Netherlands is so severe partly because it is such a public and collective matter, in which feeling at home for the native Dutch population seems to have become conditional upon the behavior, attitudes and feelings of others. Politicians from the right to the left claim that, as long as (Muslim) immigrants do not behave like respectful guests or fully assimilate, this compromises the native Dutch population's ability to feel at home. As discussed in Chapter 5, the Netherlands is one of the most culturally homogeneous countries in Europe. This homogeneity sits very well with Dutch politicians who want their country to be a home for a single, large, harmonious and progressive family. In such a household, the behavior of each family member affects everyone else's sense of belonging. Feeling at home thus comes to be seen in zero-sum terms: 'their' arrival has correspondingly reduced 'our' ability to feel at home. In the Netherlands, the individual, private home has become the conceptual framework for the nation, thus denying the heterogeneity of its citizens. The Dutch nation becomes 'a collective representation that invokes the common identity of the whole as a trump card against the internal differentiation of identities and interests' (Calhoun, 1999, p. 223). Or, as Massey and Jess put it: 'The effort...to actually make "culture" and "place" correspond with one another turns out to be a hopeless, expensive and sometimes violent and dangerous illusion' (2003, p. 186).

In the US, while the familiar/familial home is missed, the emancipation of women is seen by most Americans as an achievement and as the result of their own, individual choices. Americans (and certainly American women) supported the change; it did not just happen to them (a sentiment that dominates sensibilities in the Netherlands regarding immigration). Most Americans thus do not feel they have to blame others; 'if we want to have better homes', Americans tell each other endlessly in public and political debate, 'we have to become better parents'. The reflective nostalgia prominent in the US thus recognizes that something has indeed been lost, but that much has also been gained – and that though what has been lost is gone, better family lives may return under new conditions.

Of course the US knows less reflective forms of nostalgia as well: witness the culture wars surrounding abortion, homosexuality, gun ownership, etc. In these conflicts, some groups – for example, supporters of the Tea Party movement – clearly have revanchist agendas based on the opposition between 'the people' and the Democratic 'elite' in Washington. Though this may resemble the divide in Western Europe between the new populist parties and the 'leftwing elites', the Tea Party's ideas about national identity and minorities are radically different from their European counterparts. Due to the particular history of the US, the idea of a homogeneous country is politically untenable, at least since the civil rights movement. While political polarization can create gridlock, this is still preferable to the dangerous majority–minority split in Western Europe.

In contrast, nostalgia in the Netherlands has a strongly restorative character. In the public and political debate, many claim that all recent social change has been for the worse. 'Some people' (the accusing finger is often pointed at 'the left church') have made the wrong collective decisions, which have affected the entire Dutch public. The revanchist nostalgia is, moreover, based on a notion of territorial rights: 'we were here first'. Chronology then becomes hierarchy: it gives the native Dutch the right to prescribe to new immigrants how they must behave. But this move from chronology to hierarchy is, for various reasons, not possible in the US. Even the recent controversy over Latino immigrants centers on the economic effects of immigration (taking 'our' jobs) and not so much on the loss of cultural or national integrity.

The restoration of the 'old' Netherlands entails appreciating its national history, which all must learn. It is often claimed that immigrants in particular would benefit from a greater knowledge of Dutch history, facilitated by a shared canon or a national historical museum (Scheffer, 2007). But in the current political climate, it is the native Dutch who most value the orientation provided by a clearly spelled-out national past. It gives them the opportunity to defend their locale against newcomers, who don't share its past.

Four spheres of belonging

People in our days of heightened mobility and more fluid gender roles have responded in different ways to what they experience as their 'crisis of home'. Some have retreated into their *private* worlds, a version of defensive localism that fits the idea of home-as-haven (a common response to rapid social change in the US). In Europe, globalization has elicited other kinds of defensive localism. In the Netherlands, 'feeling at home' has transcended the private realm to become a *public* category: immigrants are forced to choose the Dutch identity, to give up old loyalties (Connor, 2007), habits, norms and values, to feel at home in their country of residence and to publicly prove it. The Dutch nation, rooted in the imaginary past, is constructed in opposition to the outside world of migration and mobility.

But there was and is more to feelings of home than being attached to either the individual home or the nation. In Chapter 1, I introduced a three-level scheme: the micro level of the household, the meso level of the community and the macro level of the nation. However, reality is more complex than this three-layered model. First of all, the three levels are inter-related. To give just two examples: in the US, the idea of a besieged 'private' home is increasingly constructed in the context of threats posed by the outside world (from the financial crisis to terrorism, see Low, 2008). In the Netherlands, the nation is constructed as a family home where migrants are the disobedient children spoiling the home feelings of 'rooted' generations. The three-level model also overlooks the place where more and more Americans feel at home: the workplace. We may thus be better off distinguishing between four spheres: the sphere of the *individual household*, the *economic* sphere of the workplace, the *associational* sphere of the community and, finally, the *politico-cultural* sphere of the nation-state.

What, then, are the characteristics of 'feeling at home' in these four spheres? Although we encountered various meanings of feeling at home, we saw that *familiarity* with places and people was extremely important for all those longing to belong. As the many examples in this book have shown, most of us are able, over time, to cultivate bonds of familiarity with different places and people. Nevertheless, familiarity is not enough. To truly feel at home, *homogeneity* (of both people and places) plays a key role. Within individual households, and to a lesser extent within communities, a certain homogeneity already prevails: one feels at home with one's own people (however defined) in one's own place (be it particular, generic and/or symbolic). But in the workplace, and even more so in the nation-state, one has to deal with *heterogeneity*. In private life and in associations one can usually choose with whom to socialize; in the economic and politico-cultural spheres one necessarily encounters pluriformity.

There is a further structuring aspect to these four spheres. Whereas the associational and the political spheres are by their nature *public* and *collective*, the economic and household spheres are more *individual* and *private*. Employees generally do not publicly or collectively feel at home in their workplaces, while the significance of associations often lies in their public visibility and collective character. Table 6.1 summarizes these aspects in broad strokes.

Table 6.1   The four spheres of 'home'

	Individual/private	Collective/public
Homogeneous	Household *Private sphere*	Community *Associational sphere*
Heterogeneous	Workplace *Economic sphere*	Nation-State *Politico-cultural sphere*

At home in the US? Feeling at home in the private and economic spheres

We saw in Chapter 1 that Americans have long been a mobile people: on average they move twice as often as Europeans and over greater distances. While the need to feel at home somewhere is as real for Americans as it is for their more sedentary European counterparts, what this home means has been greatly influenced by the history of mobility within the United States and the experience of migration to the new world. Though the rate of mobility seems to be decreasing (Fischer, 2010) as Americans finally settle down (Pew Research Center, 2008), restlessness and rootlessness are deeply rooted in the American psyche (Jasper, 2000). Feeling at home – recalling Christopher Lasch's well-known dictum 'Home is as a haven in a heartless world' – is experienced primarily in one's own house, an oasis in a turbulent and volatile world.

In practice, this house can be in different places – home can move several times over the course of one's life. To feel at home is thus not about being rooted in a specific spot or to be attached to a certain neighborhood. Home is rather a stop on a life route which promises constant change (Anderson, 1991 [1983]; Gustafson, 2001; Hannerz, 1996). Familiar, particular people and goods can aid this process of feeling at home, as can familiar, generic chains like Starbucks and McDonalds.

The ability to move repeatedly and to feel at home in new places has become part of the American identity. It fits with this adaptability that new immigrants to the US do not remain outsiders for long; they quickly become fellow Americans (Ghorashi, 2003, pp. 221–2). Although a certain exclusion of Muslim immigrants occurred after 9/11, the negative politicization of Islam in the form and intensity it took in the Netherlands and other highly secularized Western European countries did not take place. This is not to say that nothing has changed. After 9/11 the US experienced a wave of intense patriotism in which the connection was made between 'home' and 'nation'. Suddenly there was much talk of the 'homeland' (materializing in the Department of Homeland Security). Prior to 9/11, 'home' had not been associated with the nation; 'home' was at home.

The hyper-mobile American society was built on the foundation of traditional gender roles. If people moved, it was because the man had found a new job. American women (and certainly white middle-class women) were, until the 1950s, the primary home-makers. This has, of course, changed, and the American crisis of home has everything to do with (the uneven outcomes of) this gender revolution. American women, certainly in comparison to their Dutch counterparts, entered the labor force en masse. But as men did not become equal partners in the household, the emancipation of women put life at home under great stress. As elaborated in Chapter 3, the American sociologist Arlie Hochschild has described this process in a number of books, including *The Second Shift* (1989) and *The Time Bind: When Work Becomes Home and Home Becomes Work* (1997). Americans today live under permanent time pressure: they not only combine full-time jobs and family responsibilities (especially women), but also, in the lower segment of the labor market, often combine several jobs. Many Americans endure long commutes and couples are sometimes forced to live apart due to their work. For many children there is at best something curious called 'quality time'.

The uneven outcomes of the gender revolution – resulting in a destabilization of the nuclear family unsupported by welfare state provisions such as public childcare – has created a chronic time bind at home which strongly colors the American public and political debate. The crisis at home also fuels the nostalgia discussed above: in the not-too-distant past, there seemed to be much more time. 'Family values' are so popular in America today precisely because family life is under siege. In this sense, America is a nostalgic nation, a country wrestling with a revolution that has already taken place.

As we saw in Chapter 3, some Americans look to examples in Northwestern Europe for solutions to their crisis at home. Especially in the Scandinavian countries, the time bind appears less daunting due to quality public childcare and a better balance between the cost of living and the number of hours households must work. The American work-and-care debate shows that a certain type of nostalgia need not be at odds with innovation; visions for the future can grow out of appreciation for aspects of the past, as well as for how things are done in other societies. There appear to be better ways to combine work and care, and places where people have more time. There is a world to be won.

But what kind of world would that be? And what would 'home' be within it? American sociologists have been seeking to regain, where possible, some of the former aspects of home without throwing out the achievements of women's emancipation. As discussed in Chapter 3, incompatible views compete here. At one end of the spectrum, 'home' for Arlie Hochschild is a haven in a hostile, commercialized world; her view is rather nostalgic for feeling at home is to be exclusively experienced at home. At the other end of the spectrum, Dalton Conley's conception of home stretches it from the private into the economic sphere. Conley advocates a world where the barriers between the worlds of care and work no longer exist, where people will be parents at work and workers at home.

In other words, while both Hochschild and Conley acknowledge the importance of 'home', they draw disparate conclusions regarding where it should be. Whereas Hochschild claims that the only way to save home is by protecting households from the market, Conley argues that home will need to thrive in a world globalized by the internet, laptops, cell phones and other technological innovations that do not respect the old boundaries between the private sphere and the market. Home-making practices, for Conley, can take place everywhere, particularly at work. Private enterprises like Google embody the future of home.

In answering the question 'How should we balance the strong feelings of belonging many Americans have developed at work and the decline of such feelings at home?', it would be fruitful to examine other alternatives that honor the divergent preferences of people of different ages, household situations, classes and incomes, cultural backgrounds and sexualities (Coontz, 1997). Hochschild, however, seems to suggest that feeling at home-at-work and at home is a zero-sum game. But why must this be so? Her finding that for some men and women, home-at-work has replaced home-at-home does not mean that all people are unable to experience a sense of belonging in both. Perhaps surprisingly, Conley shares the same assumption: for him, feeling at home-at-work will eventually replace feeling at home-at-home – a comparable zero-sum perspective on home feelings that does scant justice to the variety of home feelings we encountered in this book.

In terms of the Table 6.1, both Hochschild and Conley focus on the shift from home-at-home to home-at-work within the 'individual/ private' pillar (that people may also feel at home within communities or within the nation is not their primary concern). An important difference is that Hochschild locates 'real' home feelings in the homogeneous environment of the individual household: home is *a private haven located in a particular place*, with strong boundaries from the economic sphere of work.[1] Note that, for Conley as well, feeling at home is an exclusive emotion (not really public, let alone collective). Home is a safe haven (parents can look after their children all day) though not a place for retreat or domesticity. And since Conley claims that we can feel at home in the workplace, 'home' is not a very particular place. Interestingly, Conley combines the idea of a *private haven* with a *generic place* as embodied in offices (though workers may try to 'particularize' their office spaces by bringing pictures of their loved ones, plants, etc.).

In this discussion of the pros and cons of these two types of 'private' homes, I propose being particularly mindful of the possible exclusionary consequences of where one locates home. If we prefer private-sphere homes to be safe havens, we know from experience that we will select 'people like us'. In the workplace we necessarily have to deal with more diversity, a significant fact in countries such as the US, where other spheres such as housing and education are highly segregated. This heterogeneity also explains why home-making at work is no easy task. In this sense, it is quite an achievement that some Americans do feel at home-at-work: it either shows that workplaces are, in fact, quite segregated or (a more optimistic reading) that some people can feel at home with others, even when they are quite different. While feeling at home, for Conley, may be a less intense emotion than it is for Hochschild, it shows the capacity of some people to attach to generic places and relative strangers.

At home in the Netherlands? Feeling at home in the politico-cultural sphere

As sketched above, the Netherlands is also experiencing nostalgic times; politicians and public opinion leaders claim a crisis in 'feeling at home' so strong that the government has made it a national policy objective: 'The goal must be to establish a society in which everybody can feel at home' (Dutch Cabinet, 2008). This crisis of home feelings in the Netherlands, and more broadly in Western Europe, has little to do with the emancipation of women (or the lack of men's emancipation), but with that other major transformation of our times: the increased global mobility of goods and, especially, people.

When Dutch politicians speak of a crisis in 'feeling at home', they are referring to increasingly immigrant neighborhoods, the lack of uniformity in social conventions, and public expressions of religiosity in a predominantly secular society. The Netherlands, imagined as a single house, 'is being taken over by foreigners'. In response, many native Dutch long for a time when it was still 'just us'. The leader of the rightwing populist party in the Netherlands, Geert Wilders, formulates his revanchism as follows: 'Millions of Dutchmen want change. They want to be proud of their country. They want to feel safe in their country again. They want another Netherlands. They want to feel at home in their own country. They want a decent and social Netherlands. They want their Netherlands back' (Dutch Parliament [Tweede Kamer], 2008b).

Wilders' is not an isolated voice in Western Europe, where the public discussion on 'feeling at home' has grown increasingly exclusionary. As 'thick', historically rooted national identities are invoked to increase cohesion within societies, the obligation to feel at home becomes particularly problematic for immigrants. The historical obsession not only requires the past to be rewritten to project all kinds of valued 'national' characteristics; it marginalizes new immigrants. The historical rooting of contemporary citizenship also encourages the belief among native populations that they naturally have the most right to feel at home.

In his book *The Perils of Belonging: Autochthony, Citizenship, and Exclusion in Africa and Europe* (2009), the anthropologist Peter Geschiere examines how 'autochthony' is used to deny (or worse, rescind) equal rights to newcomers and immigrants. The constructed primordial right to belong has an appeal of naturalness to many people (Geschiere, 2004; Geschiere and Ceuppens, 2005; Geschiere and Nyamnjoh, 2000). Note that this 'nativism' is not only alive on the political right. Many leftwing parties also have positive understandings of 'rootedness', as was evident among spokespersons of the Dutch Labor party quoted in Chapter 5. Historically, this may be understandable: the left sympathized with native populations displaced at the time of colonization by white Westerners. Progressive circles tend to have solidarity with the 'indigenous people' – problematic, however, when this solidarity is based on the idea that natives have territorial rights solely due to their status as the first inhabitants (Jackson, 1995).

The Left, at least in Western Europe, seems deeply divided on whether such historical claims to territory are justified. Does it make sense in the face of globalization to stick to such notions of entitlement and the idea that one 'belongs' in only one place? At the same time, the mobility of others strengthens historical claims among non-mobile populations. Numerous studies have shown how districts change through the influx of immigrants and the resulting assertion by native populations of 'primordial bonds' and 'rights to the ground' (Avila, 2004; Kasinitz and Hillyard, 1995; Rieder, 1985; Seligman, 2005). I fully agree with David Harvey that we need to take these 'defensive' sentiments seriously: 'The depiction of others' geographical loyalties as banal and irrational ... helps foster ignorance of and disinterest in the lives of those others' (2000, p. 556).

In the culturalist conceptualization of the Dutch nation (Duyvendak *et al.*, 2010; Schinkel, 2008, 2010; Uitermark, 2010), however, the national 'home' should be closed to newcomers who bring heterogeneity, loss of cohesion and feelings of alienation.

'Home' here is a very particular understanding of the nation, as if (in terms of the table) the politico-cultural sphere can be equated with the sphere of the homogeneous and private individual household. But this is exactly what populist politicians want: they oppose supranational entities (like the EU) and want the Netherlands to be a 'gated community' rather than a place connected to other places in countless ways. In their rhetoric, there is no place for such inconvenient facts such as there are few countries in the world where so many goods flow in and out; where such a large part of the population keeps in touch with the world online; where so many share solidarity with so many others elsewhere in the world; where so many holidays are spent overseas; where almost all citizens master two or more languages; where science is so internationally oriented; and, indeed, where so many immigrants have recently come to live. Populist politicians – so central in the debate in the Netherlands and more generally in Western Europe – fail to understand that the politico-cultural sphere is not only collective and public in nature but must also be open to a heterogeneous citizenry.

There are, to be sure, many ways to deal with this diversity in the public sphere. Some countries have tried to banish from it all particularities. This French Jacobin 'model' holds that only neutral public spaces can guarantee social peace and that deeply ingrained feelings of belonging have to remain restricted to private life. Nevertheless, such quasi-neutral spaces often bear the hallmarks of the dominant culture. The recent debates on national identity in France once more show, like earlier discussions on the headscarf, that what is presented as 'neutral' is an expression of the norms, values, attitudes and behavior of the native majority (Akan, 2009; Bertossi, 2009; Bertossi and Duyvendak, 2009; Butler, 2008). From this perspective, the secular French and Dutch anti-multicultural positions are, in fact, quite similar, though in France the secular elite still claims to be 'neutral'.

Another way of dealing with diversity in the politico-cultural sphere is to give different groups certain rights. This can come in various forms, ranging from 'thin' to 'thick' versions of multiculturalism. However, all versions of multiculturalism share a fundamental problem: if people develop thick public notions of home by celebrating their identities, they risk jeopardizing the home feelings of others. Put differently, the wish to feel completely at home in public may eventually lead to clashes between groups whose expressions of feeling at home are not (fully) compatible.

Populist nationalism is the thickest variant of the public and collective version of home: the majority claims the nation-state as its property and demands from the minority that it adapts (or disappears). This 'heaven' concept of the nation is a de facto negation of the heterogeneity of the politico-cultural sphere – and as such the end of democratic politics. Before introducing a more plural notion of 'home' befitting the politico-cultural sphere – home as a *hybrid* place – we turn to the nature of home in the associational sphere.

At home in the community? Feeling at home in the associational sphere

Communities often thrive on the basis of deep-seated feelings and historically rooted experiences. Not all communities, however, feel the same regarding their 'rights to the ground'. Many residents of smaller villages may (still) find it self-evident that they morally own the ground; in the big cities, similar claims of 'moral property' often seem out of place. This is not to say that urban communities – people who have resided in urban neighborhoods for generations – don't have claims based on place attachment (van der Graaf, 2009). But they know that these claims are necessarily relative in an urban context of constant change.

How relative such claims should be is a central motif within urban contestation. In Chapter 1, I showed that the home-making strategies of 'rooted' people often rely on attachments to *particular* places and goods. As their living environments are irrevocably affected by globalization, people seek home-making strategies that particularize their surroundings, thereby helping them to feel publicly and collectively at home (in 'heaven'). It is precisely those groups who feel socially marginalized – such as residents of disadvantaged neighborhoods or gays and lesbians – who have the greatest need for particular public places to feel at home.

But as we saw in the two examples of 'positive' home-making in Chapter 4, the search for more inclusive neighborhoods is no easy task. For the disabled, the indifference of 'normal' society meant that they ended up living isolated in their own homes (an extreme form of home-as-haven). In the case of the Castro, gays and lesbians were able to create their own particular gay district (home-as-heaven). But, as is often the case with such publicly expressed homes, the profiled identity left little room for other identities. Heterosexuals, Starbucks and the cable car were not welcome – or at least their arrival was heavily contested.

Alongside the question of how to deal with diversity *within* communities and neighborhoods, there is the further question of how relatively homogeneous communities relate to the broader urban context. Research by Kasinitz *et al.* (2008) has shown that second-generation immigrants in New York City do well partly because they live in environments that value diversity. They show that a certain homogeneity in the residential environment – in terms of ethnicity, class, age, lifestyles or sexuality – need not obstruct exchanges with others elsewhere in the city, for example in schools, in public spaces or at work. Contact with relative strangers need not diminish one's sense of belonging to the extent that one feels supported 'at home' by a rather homogeneous and nurturing community.

Such is the idea behind San Francisco's self-understanding as a 'city of communities'. It shows that getting everyone to feel at home is also a question of scale – of balancing feelings of belonging that require familiar surroundings with openness towards others living elsewhere in the city. Neighborhoods inhabited primarily by members of a single ethnic (or sexual, age or class) group can aid residents' sense of belonging.[2] The question is whether such particular places can also help their residents to live with diversity in the rest of the city, or whether they are destined to be 'defensive' places set up to keep others out.

A certain visibility of one's own group in public space can make it easier to bridge the distance with other groups. This happens most easily, for example in New York City, where everyone is a minority and power differences between groups are relatively limited. But active pluriformity to allow everyone to feel at home in public remains a delicate balancing act as manifestations of one group's feelings of home may be met by hostility from other groups.

How much space different groups should enjoy to collectively manifest their sense of belonging – on streets and squares, in schools and other public spaces, in their neighborhoods or in the city at large – remains a burning issue. Because different groups express feelings of home differently, it is idle to demand that everyone behave in the same way. Space for the public expression of feeling at home by different groups, however, only emerges when citizens empathize with the desire of others to belong. This empathy can only arise in situations where everybody's right to feel at home is respected; in order to really be able to belong somewhere, others have to agree that you belong. The basis of a harmonious society is therefore not forced assimilation into one notion of 'home' but recognition that everybody wishes to belong.

People will withdraw into their private homes if this acknowledgment is lacking (Putnam, 2007). Some may applaud such a development as it reduces public confrontations over 'who belongs'. Nevertheless, the *my house is my home* strategy (as discussed in Chapter 1) will eventually fail. The blurring of the private and public spheres will not cease by declaring public home feelings to be out of place. Home feelings for many people are neither private nor individual: they want to collectively and publicly express and experience 'home'. This need not be problematic so long as citizens do not claim the entire street, neighborhood, city or nation as their own. People can publicly and collectively express their home feelings in so far as they acknowledge that their experience of particular, generic or symbolic places as home is just one and not the only possible way. Moreover, their 'right' to feel at home – not a formal but a moral right – comes with a corresponding duty: to help others to feel at home as well.

In other words, the public sphere has to be plural. In a democratic and diverse society, the 'home' of the public sphere is necessarily *hybrid*; neither a haven nor a heaven, but a place one has to share with many others. And it is precisely because 'home feelings' are no longer limited to the private and individual sphere that we need this hybrid conceptualization of the public and collective home. That said, the breadth of nationalist policies in Western Europe leave little space for such hybridity. The politico-cultural sphere is equated to a thick notion of home for a particular group, instead of being open to all citizens. Ideal-typically, however, the nation-state should include all of its citizens. If we want to retain the idea of the nation-as-home, it needs to be a house with many rooms.

Table 6.2   Conceptions of 'home' in the four spheres

	Individual/Private	Collective/Public
Homogeneous	Household *Private Sphere* Haven/Particular place	Community *Associational Sphere* Heaven/Particular place
Heterogeneous	Workplace *Economic Sphere* Haven/Generic place	Nation-State *Politico-Cultural Sphere* Hybrid/Symbolic place

Feeling at home 'light'

Sociologists have long attempted to comprehend the importance of belonging. While many sociologists have nurtured inborn sympathies for the 'rootless' and 'restless' (see Chapter 1), others have critically analyzed the struggle between *Gesellschaft* and *Gemeinschaft* (Tönnies) and the effects of modernization (Weber's anomie). But overall, sociological studies have examined social *change* as a normative phenomenon. In broad strokes, the discipline has been future-oriented, optimistic and progressive (and hence often partisan). However, if we want to better understand the great changes of our time and the 'liquidity' of the societies (Bauman, 2007) in which we live, we as sociologists have to reconsider our repertoires. We indeed need to better comprehend the gender and migration revolutions, for they now seem to be inciting nostalgia rather than propelling us forwards. The present volume has shown that the old questions of social cohesion, of *Gemeinschaft*, and of 'home' remain current in our postmodern days of change, mobility and migration. I fully agree with Rapport and Dawson that 'while it may sometimes come laden with reactionary resonances, "home" should not be ceded to the political Right' (1998, p. 8). Or in the words of Iris Marion Young: 'The appropriate response... is not to reject the values of home, but instead to claim those values for everyone' (2005, p. 151).

One of my main conclusions concerns the political role of nostalgia. The nostalgic mood sweeping Western Europe frames the past – the national past – as the 'rooted' basis for national identity. The historical rooting of contemporary citizenship encourages the belief among native populations that they naturally have the most right to feel at home while marginalizing new immigrants who were never part of that history. 'Nostalgia' is part and parcel of the current politics of home.

Other social scientists, including anthropologists, historians and social geographers, have addressed the power of nostalgia. Urban sociology has long paid attention to feelings of 'expropriation' and 'loss' through gentrification and urban renewal – think of the well-known article by Marc Fried (1963), 'Grieving for a Lost Home'. From a more general sociological perspective, Fred Davis's *Yearning for Yesterday: A Sociology of Nostalgia* (1979) remains of interest, while Pickering and Keightley have argued that nostalgia – beautifully described as 'the composite feeling of loss, lack, and longing' (Pickering and Keightley, 2006, p. 921) – tells a story about the present as much as it does about the past. Here they come close to the works of Svetlana Boym, who does not ask what the 'real' past was (let alone the past that the nostalgics wish to reveal); instead, she examines how depictions of the past are used for the present. We need to further develop a sociology of nostalgia that understands grief for what has been lost, but also what drives this nostalgia, whom it includes and excludes, and what kinds of shared future may emerge – an empathic sociology that understands why people need to belong while showing the conditions under which they can peacefully do so.

Doreen Massey sketches the contours of a perspective on (urban) space that honors people's existing feelings of attachment without excluding newcomers:

> In this interpretation, what gives a place its specificity is not some long internalized history but the fact that it is constructed out of a particular constellation of social relations, meeting and weaving together at a particular locus. ... Instead then of thinking about places as areas with boundaries around them, they can be imagined as articulated moments in networks of social relations and understandings. ... And this in turn allows a sense of place which is extroverted, which includes a consciousness of its links with the wider world, which integrate in a positive way the global and the local. (Massey, 2007, pp. 154–5)

This switch from a *temporal* to an open, *spatial* perspective is very welcome in today's Western Europe. Nationalist conceptions of space, however, are not only exclusionary due to their historical rooting; their thick notions of home produce many 'others' as well. Nationalists – even when their nationalism is based on demanding adherence to liberal, progressive values (Lægaard, 2007; van Reekum, 2010) – leave no space for 'others' to publicly and collectively feel at home in the politico-cultural sphere.

Feeling at home is a sentiment that has its appropriate and even necessary place in the politico-cultural sphere. To be inclusive, this 'home' needs to be open and hybrid in its symbols – necessary to peacefully accommodate different feelings of home in the public arena. Moreover, the politico-cultural sphere needs to balance the shadow sides of exclusionary individual, private and homogeneous forms of belonging. In this sense, the household, economic and associational spheres rely on the political sphere, the only sphere that can truly be inclusive in terms of collectively and publicly feeling at home in a heterogeneous setting. Feeling at home in the nation-state, then, is the capacity to experience comfort among relative strangers. This does not equal the footloose cosmopolitan dream – it is the daily reality of an ever-growing group of grounded people living their home feelings 'lightly'.

Notes

1 A Homesick World?

1. Like the universalist position, this label is used to describe an empirical rather than normative position. Particularists disagree among each other, as do universalists.
2. Others, while agreeing with the latter claim, would emphasize that this longing for homogeneous space will lead to something akin to apartheid.
3. At which point the generic becomes the particular.
4. As Doreen Massey (1995) has argued, this is pertinent to many cosmopolitans: they can have their free-floating lifestyles because others are there to take care of their particular places. One of her most telling examples comes from her study of a group of highly successful male scientists at Cambridge University. 'These men are able to counterbalance the intense, virtual and actual forms of mobility of their professional lives (in which they daily communicate with colleagues internationally and regularly travel to conferences abroad) with the quieter delights of their secluded domestic lifestyles, in their houses in the Cambridgeshire countryside – which are, of course, maintained for them, in their absence, by their wives. Certainly, one of the other dimensions of differences involved here involves the way in which the burden of *Heimat* is often carried by the female "home-maker", in so far as relations to mobility and sedentarism are commonly gendered in one way or another' (pp. 190–1).

2 Why Feeling at Home Matters

1. See also annotated surveys such as Perkins and Thorns (2003).
2. Methodologically, the way to proceed is to ask when, why and where people do *not* feel at home.
3. Nowicka seems hesitant to draw the radical conclusion that 'home' can be completely de-territorialized since she – in line with the actor–network tradition she is sympathetic to – wants to emphasize the *material* side of 'home-making'. If home can be completely 'de-territorialized', how then to understand home-making practices which need to take place somewhere? While examining the material side of such an elusive concept as 'home' is laudable, it does not follow that people cannot also feel at home in non-material, non-territorialized 'worlds'.

4. This fits with Heidegger's thinking about home: 'What is it to feel a sense of belonging rather than alienation? In his answer, [Heidegger] suggested that it is a process of communication. Each generation leaves symbols and stories, rooted in time and space. Those of us in subsequent generations learn to belong by receiving and reinterpreting those stories, as well as adding our own' (Atkins, 2003, p. 10).

3   Losing Home at Home: When Men and Women Feel More at Home at Work

1. In which she writes: 'One excellent way to raise the value of care is to involve fathers in it. If men shared the care of family members worldwide, care would spread laterally instead of being passed down a social class ladder. ... For indeed it is men who have for the most part stepped aside from caring work, and it is with them that the "care drain" truly begins' (2003, p. 29).
2. This is also evident in Chris Carrington's (1999) book *No Place Like Home: Relationships and Family Life Among Lesbians and Gay Men*. Carrington writes that the unequal distribution of tasks inside and outside the home, which he also encounters among lesbian and gay male couples, has nothing to do with gender (since both partners are of the same sex). He shows that extremely egalitarian ideals exist in homosexual relationships regarding the distribution of household chores and, increasingly often, childcare tasks, with both partners attached to life at home, to 'domesticity'. Nevertheless, the two partners often contribute unequally. How is this possible? Carrington agrees with Hochschild, Gornick and Meyers, and Jacobs and Gerson, that pressure from outside – as expressed in the overpowering need for (more) money – leads to the unequal distribution of the second shift, which is performed mainly by the partner with lower income: 'Paid employment exerts the greatest influence upon the division of domesticity in most lesbigay families. The number of hours paid work requires, where the work takes place, the length of the commute to work, the pay, the prestige, and difficulty of the work all conflate to encourage a pattern of specialization. The relative resources that each person brings to the relationship from paid work influence the division of labor. In most cases, the person with less earning capacities, or with less occupational prestige, picks up a disproportionate share of domestic labor' (p. 188).
3. These figures are for 2009.
4. These figures are for 2005.
5. Some American women begin to work part time after the birth of their first child. According to Gerson and Jacobs: 'The reduced time among working parents is not gender neutral, however. Indeed, husbands work more hours when they have children at home, and their

working hours increase along with the number of children' (2004a, p. 49).

6. A person is deemed to be economically independent in the Netherlands if he or she earns 70 percent of the net minimum wage.

7. On the other hand, the situation for women is even worse in South European countries. Women in Greece and Spain, for example, spend 69.8 and 67.9 hours, respectively, on work and care, which is considerably more than women in North European countries. This is because they both work more (poor leave arrangements) and care more (poor child day care).

5 Feeling at Home in the Nation? Understanding Dutch Nostalgia

1. Pillarization refers to the division of Dutch society into religious and ideological groups during the first half of the twentieth century. There was a Roman Catholic 'pillar', a Protestant pillar that was further divided internally and a neutral or secular pillar. Each had its own schools, societies, political parties, broadcasting organizations, newspapers, hospitals, etc. This vertical split ran through all social classes.

2. The standard deviation of a series of numbers can be understood as their average distance from the average. For example, if the average result of two examinations is five, this can mean that a five was obtained in both examinations or that the respective scores were one and nine. In the first case the standard deviation is zero; in the second it is four.

3. In any election year, sentences and phrases within party programs are coded for 56 separate issues. The space devoted to each is expressed as a percentage. Polarization over authoritarianism is measured by determining the space allotted by each party to the maintenance of law and order, and then subtracting that devoted to minority groups of a non-economic and non-demographic nature. This gives each party a score reflecting how strongly it stresses authoritarianism over libertarianism. We then calculate the polarization between the parties for each election year using the standard deviation. We measure polarization over moral traditionalism by determining the space allotted to negative comments on traditional moral themes such as family, religion and immoral behavior, and then subtracting that devoted to positive comments on these issues. The resulting scores show the extent to which parties value traditional moral values. The standard deviation for each election year reflects the degree of polarization.

4. In response to the Scientific Council for Government Policy's report 'Identification with the Netherlands' (for analysis of this data, see Scientific Council for Government Policy [Wetenschappelijke Raad voor het Regeringsbeleid], 2007).

6   Conclusion: Inclusive Ways of Feeling at Home?

1. See, on negotiating these boundaries between home and work, the beautiful book by Nippert-Eng (1996).
2. While American readers may wonder why it is even necessary to point this out (see Abrahamson, 2005 [1996]), in Western Europe 'mixed neighborhoods' have become something of a policy dogma.

Bibliography

Abdelhandy, D. (2008) Representing the homeland: Lebanese diasporic notions of home and return in a global context. *Cultural Dynamics*, 20, 53–72.

Abrahamson, M. (2005 [1996]) *Urban Enclaves: Identity and Place in America*. New York: St Martin's Press.

Achterberg, P. (2006) The end of left versus right: reality or popular mythos? [Het einde van links en rechts: realiteit of populaire mythe?]. *People and Society [Mens and Maatschappij]*, 1, 51–63.

Adam, B. D., Duyvendak, J. W. and Krouwel, A. (eds) (1999) *The Global Emergence of Gay and Lesbian Politics: National Imprints of a Worldwide Movement*. Philadelphia: Temple University Press.

Advisory Committee for Refugee Affairs (2008) *Dual Nationality and Integration [Dubbele nationaliteit en integratie]*. The Hague: Sociaal en Cultureel Planbureau.

Ahmed, S. (1999) Home and away: Narratives of migration and estrangement. *International Journal of Cultural Studies*, 2(3), 329–47.

Aisenbrey, S., Evertsson, M. and Grunow, D. (2009) Is there a career penalty for mothers' time out? A comparison of Germany, Sweden, and the United States. *Social Forces*, 88(2), 573–605.

Akan, M. (2009) Laïcité and multiculturalism: the Stasi report in context. *British Journal of Sociology*, 60(2), 237–56.

Alesina, A. and Glaeser, E. (2004) *Fighting Poverty in the US and Europe: A World of Difference*. Oxford: Oxford University Press.

Anderson, B. (1991 [1983]) *Imagined Communities: Reflections on the Origin and Spread of Nationalism*. London: Verso.

Andrews, H. (2005) Feeling at home: Embodying Britishness in a Spanish charter tourist resort. *Tourist Studies*, 5(3), 247–66.

Appadurai, A. (1990) Disjuncture and difference in the global cultural economy. *Public Culture*, 2(2), 1–24.

Appiah, K. W. (1998) Cosmopolitan patriots. In P. Cheah and B. Robbins (eds), *Cosmopolitics: Thinking and Feeling beyond the Nation*. Minneapolis: University of Minnesota Press, 91–114.

Armstrong, E. A. (2002) *Forging Gay Identities: Organizing Sexuality in San Francisco, 1950–1994*. Chicago and London: University of Chicago Press.

Arts, W., Hagenaars, J. and Halman, L. (eds) (2003) *The Cultural Diversity of European Unity: Findings, Explanations and Reflections from the European Values Study*. Leiden: Brill Academic.

Atkins, G. (2003) *Gay Seattle: Stories of Exile and Belonging*. Seattle: University of Washington Press.

Avila, E. (2004) *Popular Culture in the Age of White Flight: Fear and Fantasy in Suburban Los Angeles*. Berkeley, Los Angeles and London: University of California Press.

Bauman, Z. (1998a) *Globalization: The Human Consequences*. Cambridge: Polity Press.

Bauman, Z. (1998b) *Postmodernity and its Discontents*. Cambridge: Polity Press.

Bauman, Z. (2007) *Liquid Times: Living in an Age of Uncertainty*. Cambridge: Polity Press.

Beatley, T. (2004) *Native to Nowhere: Sustaining Home and Community in a Global Age*. Washington, DC: Island Press.

Beck, U. (2000) *What Is Globalization?* Cambridge: Polity Press.

Beck, U. (2002) The cosmopolitan society and its enemies. *Theory, Culture and Society*, 19(1–2), 17–44.

Beemyn, B. (1997) *Creating a Place for Ourselves: Lesbian, Gay, and Bisexual Community Histories*. New York and London: Routledge.

Bell, A. (2010) Being 'at home' in the nation: hospitality and sovereignty in talk about immigration. *Ethnicities*, 10(2), 236–56.

Bell, L., Burtless, G., Gornick, J. and Smeeding, T. M. (2007) Failure to launch: cross-national trends in the transition to economic independence. *Luxembourg Income Study Working Paper Series*, 456.

Bell, L., & Freeman, R. B. (2001). The incentive for working hard: explaining hours worked differences in the U.S. and Germany. *Labour Economics, 8*(2), 181–202.

Berger, J. (1984) *And Our Faces, My Heart, Brief as Photos*. London: Writers and Readers.

Berger, P. L., Berger, B. and Kellner, H. (1973) *The Homeless Mind: Modernization and Consciousness*. New York: Random House.

Bertossi, C. (2009) The Republican model and its modeling discourse: performative integration in a French way [La République 'modéle' et ses discours modélisants: l'intégration performative à la française]. *Migrations' Society [Migrations Société]*, 21(122), 39–76.

Bertossi, C. and Duyvendak, J. W. (2009) Introduction: thinking the 'model', changing the question [Introduction: penser le 'modéle', changer de question]. *Migrations' Society [Migrations Société]*, 21(122), 27–37.

Blokland, T. (2003) *Urban Bonds*. Cambridge: Polity Press.

Blunt, A. and Dowling, R. (2006) *Home*. London: Routledge.

Bos, W. (2008) Modernising social democracy: back to the future, Progressive Governance Conference. London.

Bourdieu, P. (1999) *Pascalian Meditations*. Cambridge Polity Press.

Boyd, N. A. (1997) Homos invade SF! San Francisco's history as a wide-open town. In B. Beemyn (ed.), *Creating a Place for Ourselves*. New York and London: Routledge.

Boyd, N. A. (2003) *Wide Open Town: A History of Queer San Francisco to 1965*. Berkeley and Los Angeles: University of California Press.

Boym, S. (2001) *The Future of Nostalgia*. New York: Basic.

Bozkurt, E. (2009) *Conceptualising 'Home': The Question of Belonging among Turkish Families in Germany*. Frankfurt and New York: Campus Verlag.

Braidotti, R. (1994) *Nomadic Subjects: Embodiment and Sexual Difference in Contemporary Feminist Theory*. New York: Columbia University Press.

Brenner, N. (2004) *New State Spaces: Urban Governance and the Rescaling of Statehood*. New York: Oxford University Press.

Buchanan, W. (2007) SF's Castro district faces an identity crisis. *San Francisco Chronicle*, 25 February, p. 1A.

Budge, I., Klingemann, H. D., Volkens, A., Bara, J. and Tanenbaum, E. (2001) *Mapping Policy Preferences: Estimates for Parties, Electors, and Governments 1945–1998*. New York: Oxford University Press.

Buruma, I. (2006) *Murder in Amsterdam: The Death of Theo van Gogh and the Limits of Tolerance*. New York: Penguin.

Butler, J. (2008) Sexual politics, torture, and secular time. *British Journal of Sociology*, 59(1), 1–23.

Calhoun, C. (ed.) (1991) *Social Theory and the Politics of Identity*. Oxford: Blackwell.

Calhoun, C. (1998) Community without propinquity revisited: communications technology and the transformation of the urban public sphere. *Sociological Inquiry*, 68(3), 373–97.

Calhoun, C. (1999) Nationalism, political community and the representation of society. *European Journal of Social Theory*, 2(2), 217–31.

Carrington, C. (1999) *No Place Like Home: Relationships and Family Life Among Lesbians and Gay Men*. Chicago: Chicago University Press.

Castells, M. (1989) *The Informational City*. Oxford: Blackwell.

Castells, M. (1996) *The Rise of the Network Society* (Vol. 1). Massachusetts and Oxford: Blackwell.

Catalyst (2009) *2009 Catalyst Census: Fortune 500 Women Board Directors*. www.catalyst.org/file/320/2009_fortune_500_census_women_board_directors.pdf, accessed 21 October 2010.

CBS (2010) *Developments in the Economic Independence of Women. Socio-Economic Trends, 2nd Quarter 2010 [Ontwikkelingen in de economische zelf-standigheid van vrouwen. Sociaaleconomische trends, 2e kwartaal 2010]*. The Hague: Centraal Bureau voor de Statistiek.

Chabot, S. and Duyvendak, J. W. (2002) Globalization and transnational diffusion between social movements: essentialist diffusionism and beyond. *Theory and Society*, 31(6), 697–740.

Chapman, T. and Hockey, J. (eds) (1999) *Ideal Homes? Social Change and Domestic Life*. New York and London: Routledge.

City of Amsterdam (2006) We Citizens of Amsterdam II. Investing in People and Limits [Wij Amsterdammers II. Investeren in mensen en grenzen]. Amsterdam.

Clapham, D. (2005) *The Meaning of Housing: A Pathways Approach*. Bristol: Policy Press.

Collins, C. (2007) *Homeland Mythology. Biblical Narratives in American Culture*. University Park, PA: Pennsylvania State University Press.

Conley, D. (2009) *Elsewhere, USA*. New York: Pantheon.

Connor, J. (2007) *The Sociology of Loyalty*. New York: Springer.

Coontz, S. (1992) *The Way We Never Were: American Families and the Nostalgia Trap*. New York: Basic.

Coontz, S. (1997) *The Way We Really Are: Coming to Terms with America's Changing Families*. New York: Basic.

Dagevos, J., Gijsberts, M. and van Praag, C. (2003) *Report on Minorities 2003: Education, Work, and Sociocultural Integration [Rapportage minderheden 2003: Onderwijs, arbeid en sociaal-culturele integratie]*. The Hague: Sociaal en Cultureel Planbureau.

Dagevos, J., Schellingerhout, R. and Vervoort, M. (2007) Socio-cultural integration and religion [Sociaal-culturele integratie en religie]. In J. Dagevos and M. Gijsberts (eds), *Annual Report on Integration 2007 [Jaarrapport Integratie 2007]*) The Hague: Sociaal en Cultureel Planbureau, 163–92.

Damasio, A. R. (1999) Commentary by Antonio R. Damasio. *Neuro-Psychoanalysis*, 1, 38–9.

Davis, F. (1979) *Yearning for Yesterday: A Sociology of Nostalgia*. New York: Free Press.

de Gruijter, M., Smits van Waesberghe, E. and Boutellier, H. (2010) *A Foreigner in One's Own Country ['Een vreemde in eigen land']*. Amsterdam: Aksant.

de Koster, W., Achterberg, P., Houtman, D. and Van der Waal, J. (2010) Free from God: Post-Christian cultural conflict in the Netherlands [Van God los: Post-Christelijk cultureel conflict in Nederland]. *Sociology [Sociologie]*, 6(3), 27–49.

de Koster, W. and van der Waal, J. (2006) To theoretically and methodologically disentangle moral conservatism and authoritarianism: on cultural value orientations in political sociology [Moreel conservatisme en autoritarisme theoretisch en methodisch ontward: Culturele waardeoriëntaties in de politieke sociologie]. *People and Society [Mens en Maatschappij]*, 81(2), 121–41.

Demant, F. (2005) More adaptation than integration: on the cultural integration of minorities in the Netherlands and Germany [Meer aanpassing dan inpassing: over de culturele integratie van migranten in Nederland en Duitsland]. *Migrant Studies [Migrantenstudies]*, 21(2), 70–86.

Després, C. (1991) The meaning of home: literature review and directions for future research and theoretical development. *The Journal of Architectural and Planning Research*, 8(2), 96–115.

Dutch Cabinet (2008) Response of Dutch cabinet regarding WRR report 'IdentificationwiththeNetherlands' [Kabinetsstandpunt Wetenschappelijke Raad voor het Regeringsbeleid-rapport Identificatie met Nederland].

Dutch Parliament [Tweede Kamer] (1983/1984) Parliamentary Papers: New Memorandum on the Mental Health Service [Nota geestelijke volksgezondheid] (Vol. 18463).

Dutch Parliament [Tweede Kamer] (1992/1993) Parliamentary Papers: In the Community: Mental Health and Mental Healthcare in a Social Perspective

[Onder anderen. Geestelijke gezondheid en geestelijke gezondheidszorg in maatschappelijk perspectief] (Vol. 23067).

Dutch Parliament [Tweede Kamer] (1996/1997) Parliamentary Papers: Mental Health Services [Geestelijke gezondheidszorg]. (Vol. 25424).

Dutch Parliament [Tweede Kamer] (1998/1999) Parliamentary Papers: Mental Health Services [Geestelijke gezondheidszorg], *Letter from the Minister of Health, Welfare, and Sport [brief van de minister van Volksgezondheid, Welzijn en Sport]* (Vol. 25424).

Dutch Parliament [Tweede Kamer] (2000a) Parliamentary Papers: Being Dutch [Nederlanderschap].

Dutch Parliament [Tweede Kamer] (2000b) Parliamentary Papers: Public Housing, City Planning and Conservation [Volkshuisvesting, Ruimtelijke Ordening en Milieubeheer].

Dutch Parliament [Tweede Kamer] (2004) Parliamentary Papers: Report of the Blok Commission [Rapport commissie-Blok].

Dutch Parliament [Tweede Kamer] (2007) Parliamentary Papers: Declaration of the Cabinet [Regeringsverklaring].

Dutch Parliament [Tweede Kamer] (2008a) Parliamentary Papers: Fitna, 4880–921.

Dutch Parliament [Tweede Kamer] (2008b) Parliamentary Papers: Living, Neighborhoods, and Integration [Wonen, Wijken, en Integratie].

Duyvendak, J. W. (1997) *What Is Left of Government? Essays on Purple Politics, Civil Society, and Social Cohesion [Waar Blijft de Politiek? Essays over Paarse Politiek, Maatschappelijk Middenveld en Sociale Cohesie]*. Amsterdam: Boom.

Duyvendak, J. W. (1999) *The Planning of Self-Development [De Planning van Ontplooiing]*. The Hague: Sdu.

Duyvendak, J. W. (2004) *A United, Progressive Nation [Een Eensgezinde en Vooruitstrevende Natie]*. Amsterdam: Vossiuspers UvA.

Duyvendak, J. W. (2007) At home in politics? On social exclusion, self-exclusion and feeling at home in the Netherlands [Thuis in de politiek? Over sociale uitsluiting, zelfafsluiting en thuis voelen in Nederland]. In J. W. Duyvendak (ed.), *Power and Responsibility [Macht en verantwoordelijkheid]*. Amsterdam: Amsterdam University Press, 113–21.

Duyvendak, J. W. and Nederland, T. (2006) Patients in the political arena [Patiënten in de politieke arena]. *Sociology [Sociologie]*, 2(2), 178–87.

Duyvendak, J. W. and Scholten, P. (2009) Questioning the Dutch 'multicultural model' of integration [Le 'modéle multiculturel' d'intégration néerlandais en question]. *Migrations' Society [Migrations Société]*, 21(122), 77–105.

Duyvendak, J. W. and Stavenuiter, M. M. J. (2010) *Of Markets and Men: Lessons from the US and Europe for Strategies to Reach a Better Work/Life Balance*. Utrecht: Verwey-Jonker Instituut.

Duyvendak, J. W. and Verplanke, L. (2011) Strategies for sustainable movements. In W. Nicholls, J. Beaument and B. MIller (eds), *Space of Contention: Spatialities and Social Movements*. London: Ashgate.

Duyvendak, J. W., Hurenkamp, M. and Tonkens, E. (2010) Culturalization of citizenship in the Netherlands. In A. C. D'Appollonia and S. Reich (eds),

Managing Ethnic Diversity after 9/11: Integration, Security and Civil Liberties in Transatlantic Perspective. New Brunswick: Rutgers University Press, 233–52.

Duyvendak, J. W., Pels, T. and Rijkschroeff, R. (2009) A multicultural paradise? The cultural factor in Dutch integration policy. In J. L. Hochschild and J. H. Mollenkopf (eds), *Bringing Outsiders In: Transatlantic Perspectives on Immigrant Political Incorporation.* Ithaca and London: Cornell University Press, 129–39.

Duyvendak, J. W., Rijkschroeff, R., de Gruijter, M., van Daal, H. J. and Weijers, G. (2004) Self-organisations among migrants: An additional historical study of original sources on integration policy [Zelforganisaties van migranten: Aanvullend bronnenonderzoek Verwey-Jonker Instituut]. *Parliamentary Papers 28689, 12 (2003–2004),* 108–63.

Easthope, H. (2004) A place called home. *Housing, Theory and Society,* 21(3), 128–38.

Ellingsaeter, A. (1999) Dual breadwinners between state and markets. In R. Crompton (ed.), *Restructuring Gender Relations and Employment: The Decline of the Male Breadwinner.* Oxford and New York: Oxford University Press, 40–59.

Entzinger, H. and Dourleijn, E. (2008) *The Standard Gets Higher: The Life World of Youth in a Multi-ethnic City [De lat steeds hoger: De leefwereld van jongeren in een multi-etnische stad].* Assen: Van Gorcum.

Epstein, C. F., and Kalleberg, A. (eds) (2004) *Fighting for Time: Shifting Boundaries of Work and Social Life.* New York: Russell Sage Foundation.

EUMC (2002) *Report on Islamophobia after September 11.* Vienna: European Monitoring Centre on Xenophobia and Racism (EUMC).

Evans, J. M., Lippoldt, D. C. and Marianna, P. (2001) Labor market and social policy: trends in working hours in OECD countries. *Labor Market and Social Policy Occasional Paper 45.*

Feirabend, J. and Rath, J. (1996) Making a place for Islam in politics: local authorities dealing with Islamic associations. In W. A. R. Shaid and P. S. van Koningsveld (eds), *Muslims in the Margin: Political Responses to the Presence of Islam in Western Europe.* Kampen: Kok Pharos, 243–58.

Fischer, C. (1982) *To Dwell Among Friends: Personal Networks in Town and City.* Chicago: University of Chicago Press.

Fischer, C. S. (2010) *Made In America: A Social History of American Culture and Character.* Chicago and London: University of Chicago Press.

Fried, M. (1963) Grieving for a Lost Home. In L. Dulh (ed.), *The Urban Condition.* New York: Basic.

Fried, M. (2000) Continuities and discontinuities of place. *Journal of Environmental Psychology,* 20, 193–205.

Friedan, B. (1963) *The Feminine Mystique.* New York: Norton.

Frijda, N. H. (2004) Emotions and action. In A. S. R. Manstead, N. H. Frijda and A. Fischer (eds), *Feelings and Emotions: The Amsterdam Symposium.* Cambridge: Cambridge University Press, 158–73.

Fuwa, M. (2004) Macro-level gender inequality and the division of household labor in 22 countries. *American Sociological Review,* 69(6), 751–67.

Gamson, J. (1995) Must identity movements self-destruct? A queer dilemma. *Social Problems*, 42(3), 390–407.

Gerson, K. (2004a) The morality of time: women and the expanding workweek. *Dissent*, 51(4), 53–56.

Gerson, K. (2004b) Understanding work and family through a gender lens. *Journal of Community, Work, and Family*, 7(2), 163–78.

Gerson, K. and Jacobs, J. (2004) The work-home crunch. *Contexts*, 3(4), 29–37.

Geschiere, P. (2004) Ecology, belonging and xenophobia: the 1994 forest law in Cameroon and the issue of 'community'. In H. Englund and F. Nyamnjoh (eds), *Rights and the Politics of Recognition in Africa*. London and New York: Zed, 237–59.

Geschiere, P. (2009) *The Perils of Belonging: Autochthony, Citizenship, and Exclusion in Africa and Europe*. Chicago: University of Chicago Press.

Geschiere, P. and Ceuppens, B. (2005) Autochtony: local or global? New modes in the struggle over citizenship and belonging in Africa and Europe. *Annual Review of Anthropology*, 34, 385–407.

Geschiere, P. and Nyamnjoh, F. (2000) Capitalism and autochthony: the seesaw of mobility and belonging. *Public Culture*, 12(2), 423–52.

Ghorashi, H. (2003) *Ways to Survive, Battles to Win: Iranian Women Exiles in the Netherlands and the United States*. New York: Nova Science.

Giddens, A. (1991) *Modernity and Self-identity: Self and Society in the Late Modern Age*. Stanford: Stanford University Press.

Gieryn, T. (2000) A space for place in sociology. *Annual Reviews Sociology*, 26, 463–96.

Godfroy, B. J. (1988) *Neighborhoods in Transition: The Making of San Francisco's Ethnic and Nonconformist Communities*. Berkeley: University of California Press.

Goffman, E. (1961) *Asylums: Essays on the Social Situation of Mental Patients and Other Inmates*. Harmondsworth: Penguin.

Gornick, J. C. and Meyers, M. K. (2003) *Families that Work: Policies for Reconciling Parenthood and Employment*. New York: Russell Sage Foundation.

Greco, M., and Stenner, P. (eds) (2008) *Emotions. A Social Science Reader*. London: Routledge.

Gupta, A., and Ferguson, J. (1992) Beyond 'culture': space, identity, and the politics of difference. *Cultural Anthropology*, 7(1), 6–23.

Gustafson, P. (2001) Roots and routes: exploring the relationship between place attachment and mobility. *Environment and Behaviour*, 33(5), 667–86.

Gustafson, P. (2009) Mobility and territorial belonging. *Environment and Behaviour*, 41(4), 490–508.

Haas, L. and Hwang, C. P. (2007) Gender and organizational culture: correlates of companies' responsiveness to fathers in Sweden. *Gender and Society*, 21(1), 52–79.

Halman, L., Luijkx, R. and van Zundert, M. (2005) *Atlas of European Values*. Tilburg: Brill.

Hannerz, U. (1996) *Transnational Connections: Culture, People, Places*. London: Routledge.

Hareven, T. K. (1983) Review: origins of the 'modern family' in the United States. *Journal of Social History*, 17(2), 339–44.

Hareven, T. K. (1993) The home and the family in historical perspective. In A. Mack (ed.), *Home: A Place in the World*. New York and London: New York University Press, 227–60.

Harvey, D. (1989) *The Condition of Postmodernity: An Enquiry into the Origins of Cultural Change*. Oxford: Blackwell.

Harvey, D. (2000) Cosmopolitanism and the banality of geographical evils. *Public Culture*, 12(2), 529–54.

Hayden, D. (2002)*Redesigning the American Dream: Gender, Housing, and Family Life*. New York: W. W. Norton.

Hearn, J. (2007) National identity: banal, personal, and embedded. *Nations and Nationalism*, 13(4), 657–74.

Heidegger, M. (1977 [1947]) Letter on Humanism. In D. F. Krell (ed.), *Martin Heidegger's Basic Writings*. New York: Harper and Row, 193–242.

Hidalgo, M. C. and Hernandez, B. (2001) Place attachment: conceptual and empirical questions. *Journal of Environmental Psychology*, 21, 273–81.

Hochschild, A. (1983) *The Managed Heart: Commercialization of Human Feeling*. Berkeley: University of California Press.

Hochschild, A. (1989) *The Second Shift: Working Parents and the Revolution at Home*. New York: Avon.

Hochschild, A. (1997) *The Time Bind: When Work Becomes Home and Home Becomes Work*. New York: Metropolitan.

Hochschild, A. (2003) *The Commercialization of Intimate Life: Notes from Home and Work*. Berkeley: University of California Press.

Hochschild, A. (2006) Love and Gold. In D. M. Newman and J. A. O'Brien (eds), *Sociology: Exploring the Architecture of Everyday Life: Readings*. London: Sage, 212–20.

Hochschild, A. and Ehrenreich, B. (eds) (2003) *Global Woman: Nannies, Maids, and Sex Workers in the New Economy*. New York: Metropolitan.

Hollander, J. (1991) *Yearning: Race, Gender, and Cultural Politics*. London: Turnaround.

Holloway, S. L. (2008) House and home. In T. Hall, P. Hubbard and J. R. Short (eds), *The Sage Companion to the City*. Los Angeles and London: Sage.

Holy, L. (1998) The metaphor of 'home' in Czech nationalist discourse. In N. Rapport and A. Dawson (eds), *Migrants of Identity: Perceptions of Home in a World of Movement*. Oxford and New York: Berg, 111–37.

hooks, B. (2009) *Belonging: A Culture of Place*. New York and London: Routledge.

Houtman, D. and Duyvendak, J. W. (2009) Burkhas, burkhinis, and tax dollars: Cultural and political polarization in a post-Christian society [Boerka's, boerkini's en belastingcenten: Culturele en politieke polarisatie in een post-Christelijke samenleving]. In Council for Social Development [Raad voor Maatschappelijke Ontwikkeling] (ed.), *Polarisation. Threatening and Enriching [Polarisatie. Bedreigend en Verrijend].* Amsterdam: SWP, 102–19.

Houtman, D., Achterberg, P. and Duyvendak, J. W. (2008) The heated political culture of a de-pillarized society [De verhitte politieke cultuur van een ontzuilde samenleving]. In B. Snels and N. Thijssen (eds), *The Big Divide, Heated Politics in Times of Confusion [De grote Kloof. Verhitte politiek in tijden van verwarring].* Amsterdam: Uitgeverij SWP, 61–79.

Howe, A. C. (2001) Queer pilgrimage: the San Francisco homeland and identity tourism. *Cultural Anthropology*, 16(1), 35–61.

Inglehart, R. and Baker, W. E. (2000) Modernization, cultural change, and the persistence of traditional values. *American Sociological Review*, 65(1), 19–51.

Inglehart, R. and Welzel, C. (2005) *Modernization, Cultural Change, and Democracy: The Human Development Sequence.* Cambridge: Cambridge University Press.

Ireland, P. (2004) *Becoming Europe: Immigration, Integration and the Welfare State.* Pittsburgh: University of Pittsburgh Press.

Isin, E. F., Nyers, P. and Turner, B. S. (2008) *Citizenship between Past and Future.* Abingdon: Routledge.

Jackson, M. (1995) *At Home in the World.* Durham, NC: Duke University Press.

Jacobs, J. and Gerson, K. (2004a) *The Time Divide: Work, Family, and Gender Inequality.* Cambridge: Harvard University Press.

Jacobs, J. and Gerson, K. (2004b) Understanding changes in American working time: a synthesis. In C. F. Epstein and A. Kalleberg (eds), *Fighting for Time: Shifting Boundaries of Work and Social Life.* New York: Russell Sage Foundation, 25–45.

Jansen, E. (2008) Progressiveness, Uniformity and Xenophobia: The Paradox of Tolerance? [Vooruitstrevendheid, Uniformiteit en Xenofobie: Paradox van de Tolerantie?]. MA –thesis, University of Amsterdam.

Jasper, J. M. (2000) *Restless Nation: Starting Over in America.* Chicago: University of Chicago Press.

Jasper, J. M. (2006) *Getting Your Way: Strategic Dilemmas in the Real World.* Chicago and London: University of Chicago Press.

Joppke, C. (2004) The retreat of multiculturalism in the liberal state: theory and policy. *The British Journal of Sociology*, 55(2), 237–57.

Kaplan, A. (2003) Homeland insecurities: reflections on language and space. *Radical History Review*, 85, 82–93.

Kasinitz, P. and Hillyard, D. (1995) The old-timer's tale: the politics of nostalgia on the waterfront. *Journal of Contemporary Ethnography*, 24(2), 139–64.

Kasinitz, P., Mollenkopf, J. H., Waters, M. C. and Holdaway, J. (2008) *Inheriting the City: The Children of Immigrants Come of Age.* Cambridge: Harvard University Press.

Koopmans, I. and Schippers, J. (2006) The combination of paid labour and care in Europe [De combinatie van betaalde arbeid en zorg in Europa]. *B* and M, *Journal for Policy, Politics, and Society [B en M, Tijdschrift voor beleid, politiek en maatschappij]*, 33(1), 16–33.

Koopmans, R. (2002) Migrant claim-making between transnationalism and national citizenship. Amsterdam: presented at the conference Ethno-Religious Cultures, Identities and Political Philosophies (2–5 July).

Koopmans, R. and Statham, P. (2000) Migration and ethnic relations as a field of political contention: an opportunity structure approach. In R. Koopmans and P. Statham (eds), *Challenging Immigration and Ethnic Relations Politics: Comparative European Perspectives*. Oxford: Oxford University Press.

Koopmans, R., Statham, P., Giugni, M. and Passy, F. (2005) *Contested Citizenship: Immigration and Cultural Diversity in Europe*. Minneapolis: University of Minnesota Press.

Kumar, K. and Makarova, E. (2008) The portable home. *Sociological Theory*, 26(4), 324–43.

Kwekkeboom, M. H. (1999) *To everyone's capacity: explorative research on support for and the carrying capacity of community care for people with psychiatric problems [Naar draagkracht: Een verkennend onderzoek naar draagvlak en draagkracht voor de mermaatschappelijking in de ggz]*. The Hague: Sociaal en Cultureel Planbureau.

Kwekkeboom, M. H. (2001) *As Normal as Possible: Research on the Support for and the Carrying Capactity of Community Care for People with Psychiatric Problems [Zo gewoon mogelijk. Een onderzoek naar draagvlak en draagkracht voor de vermaatschappelijking in de geestelijke gezondheidszorg]*. The Hague: Sociaal en Cultureel Planbureau.

Kwekkeboom, M. H. (2004) The value of community care [De waarde van vermaatschappelijking]. *Monthly for Mental Health [Maandblad Geestelijke volksgezondheid]*, 59(6), 500–10.

Kwekkeboom, M. H. (ed.) (2006) *One's Own Home ... Experiences of People with Psychiatric or Mental Disabilities with Problems Living on their Own and Taking Part in Society [Een eigen huis ... Ervaringen van mensen met verstandelijke beperkingen of psychiatrische problemen met zelfstandig wonen en deelname aan de samenleving]*. The Hague: Sociaal en Cultureel Planbureau.

Kwekkeboom, M. H., and van Weert, C. (2008) *Participating and Being Happy. Exploratory Research on the Social Participation of People with a Mental Disability or Chronic Psychiatric Problem [Meedoen en gelukkig zijn. Een verkennend onderzoek naar de participatie van mensen met een verstandelijke beperking of chronische psychiatrische problemen]*. The Hague: Sociaal en Cultureel Planbureau.

Lægaard, S. (2007) Liberal nationalism and the nationalisation of liberal values. *Nations and Nationalism*, 13(1), 37–55.

Laing, R. D. (1960) *The Divided Self: An Existential Study in Sanity and Madness*. Harmondsworth: Penguin.

Ley-Cervantes, M. (2008) Is it a Homeless World? Home and Feelings of Home in a Group of Young Mexicans. MA –thesis, University of Amsterdam.

Leyland, W. (ed.) (2002) *Out in the Castro: Desire, Promise, Activism*. San Francisco: Leyland.

Low, S. (2004) *Behind the Gates: Life, Security, and the Pursuit of Happiness in Fortress America.* New York: Routledge.

Low, S. (2008) The New Emotions of Home: Fear, Insecurity, and Paranoia. In M. Sorkin (ed.), *Indefensible Space: The Architecture of the National Insecurity State.* London: Routledge, 233–57.

Mack, A. (ed.) (1993) *Home: A Place in the World.* New York: New York University Press.

Malkki, L. (1992) National geographic: the rooting of peoples and the territorialization of national identity among scholars and refugees. *Cultural Anthropology,* 7(1), 24–44.

Mallet, S. (2004) Understanding home: a critical review of the literature. *The Sociological Review,* 52(1), 62–89.

Mandel, H. and Semyonov, M. (2005) Family policies, wage structures, and gender gaps: sources of earnings, inequality in 20 countries. *American Sociological Review,* 70, 949–67.

Manzo, L. C. (2003) Beyond house and haven: toward a revisioning of emotional relationships with places. *Journal of Environmental Psychology,* 23, 47–61.

Marijnissen, J. (2004) Our Constitution [Onze Grondwet]. www.janmarijnissen.nl/2004/11/08/onze-grondwet/, accessed 1 October 2009.

Marijnissen, J. (writer) (2008) *Buitenhof* [Television Program]. Netherlands.

Marshall-Fratani, R. (2006) The war of 'who is who': autochthony, nationalism, and citizenship in the Ivoirian crisis. *African Studies Review,* 49(2), 9–43.

Massey, D. (1995) Places and their pasts. *History Workshop Journal,* 39, 182–92.

Massey, D. (2003) The conceptualization of space. In D. Massey & P. Jess (eds), A Place in the World? Oxford: Oxford University Press, 45–86.

Massey, D. (2007) *World City.* Cambridge: Polity Press.

Massey, D. and Jess, P. (eds) (2003) *A Place in the World?* Oxford: Oxford University Press.

Means, R. and Smith, R. (1998) *Community Care. Policy and Practice.* Basingstoke and London: Palgrave Macmillan.

Meeker, M. (2006) *Contacts Desired: Gay and Lesbian Communications and Community, 1940s–1970s.* Chicago and London: University of Chicago Press.

Mepschen, P., Duyvendak, J. W. and Tonkens, E. (2010) Sexual politics, Orientalism and multicultural citizenship in the Netherlands. *Sociology,* 44(5), 1–18.

Moore, J. (2000) Placing home in context. *Journal of Environmental Psychology,* 230, 207–17.

Morley, D. (2001) Belongings: place, space and identity in a mediated world. *European Journal of Cultural Studies,* 4(4), 425–48.

Morley, D. and Robins, K. (1995) *Spaces of Identity: Global Media, Electronic Landscapes and Cultural Boundaries.* London: Routledge.

Nippert-Eng, C. E. (1996) *Home and Work.* Chicago and London: University of Chicago Press.

Nirjé, B. (1969) The normalization principle and its human management implications. In R. Kugel and W. Wolfensberger (eds), *Changing Patterns in Residential Services for the Mentally Retarded*. Washington, DC: President's Committee on Mental Retardation, 179–95.

Nowicka, M. (2007) Mobile locations: construction of home in a group of mobile transnational professionals. *Global Networks*, 7(1), 69–86.

NRC correspondent (2010) Moroccans feel at home in the Netherlands despite negative image [Marokkaan voelt zich thuis in Nederland ondanks imago]. *NRC Handelsblad*, 29 June, p. 3.

Overkamp, E. (2000) *Institutions Move into the Neighborhood [Instellingen nemen de wijk]*. Assen: Van Gorcum.

Pamuk, A. (2004) Geography of immigrant clusters in global cities: a case study of San Francisco, 2000. *International Journal of Urban and Regional Affairs*, 28(2), 287–307.

Pateman, C. (1989) *The Disorder of Women*. Cambridge: Polity Press.

Pels, D. (1999) Privileged nomads: on the strangeness of intellectuals and the intellectuality of strangers. *Theory, Culture and Society*, 16(1), 63–86.

Perkins, H. and Thorns, D. (2003) The making of home in a global world. Aotearoa/New Zealand as an exemplar. In R. Forrest and J. Lee (eds), *Housing and Social Change: East–West Perspectives*. London: Routledge, 120–39.

Perrot, M. (1990) At home. In M. Perrot (ed.), *A History of Private Life: From the Fires of the Revolution to the Great War*. Cambridge: Harvard University Press, 341–58.

Pettit, B. and Hook, J. (2002) The structure of women's employment in comparative perspective. *Luxembourg Income Study Working Paper Series No. 330*.

Pew Research Center (2008) American mobility: Who moves? Who stays? Where's home? [Electronic version]. www.pewsocialtrends.org/assets/pdf/Movers-and-Stayers.pdf, accessed 12 October 2010.

Pickering, M. and Keightley, E. (2006) The modalities of nostalgia. *Current Sociology*, 54(6), 919–41.

Porteous, J. D. and Smith, S. E. (2001) *Domicide: The Global Destruction of Home*. Montreal and Kingston: McGill-Queen's University Press.

Powell, M. (2008) The American wanderer, in all his stripes. *The New York Times*, August, 6–7.

Preston, J. (ed.) (1991) *Hometowns: Gay Men Write About Hometowns Where They Belong*. New York: Dutton.

Putnam, R. (2007) E pluribus unum: diversity and community in the 21st century. *Scandinavian Political Studies*, 30(2), 137–74.

PvdA (2009) Political Manifesto: Labour Party [Partij van de Arbeid/ PVDA].

Quackenbush, V. (1999) Save the Castro from... 'Save the Castro', *Save the Castro Collection*. San Francisco: Can be found at: GLBT Historical Society, 657 Mission St, Suite 300, San Francisco, CA 94105.

Rapport, N., and Dawson, A. (1998) *Migrants of Identity: Perceptions of Home in a World of Movement*. Oxford: Berg.

Rath, J., Penninx, R., Groenendijk, K. and Meijer, A. (1999) The politics of recognizing religious diversity in Europe. *Netherlands Journal of Social Sciences*, 35, 53–67.

Rieder, J. (1985) *Canarsie: The Jews and Italians of Brooklyn against Liberalism.* Cambridge: Harvard University Press.

Robertson, R. (1995) Glocalization: time-space and homogeneity-heterogeneity. In M. Featherstone, S. Lash and R. Robertson (eds), *Global Modernities* London: Sage.

Robinson, J. P. and Goodbey, G. (1997) *Time for Life: The Surprising Ways Americans Use their Time.* University Park: Pennsylvania State University Press.

Rose, P. I. (ed.) (2005) *The Dispossessed: An Anatomy of Exile.* Amherst and Boston: University of Massachusetts Press.

Rosenfeld, M. J. and Byung-Soo, K. (2005) The independence of young adults and the rise of interracial and same-sex unions. *American Sociological Review*, 70, 541–62.

Rubenstein, R. (2001). Feminism, eros, and the coming of age. *Frontiers: A Journal of Women's Studies*, 22(2), 1–19.

Rybczynski, W. (1986) *Home: A Short History of an Idea.* New York: Penguin.

Said, E. (1979) Zionism from the standpoint of its victims. *Social Text*, 1, 7–58.

Sainsbury, D. (1999) *Gender, Equality, and Welfare States.* New York: Cambridge University Press.

Sandel, M. J. (1982) *Liberalism and the Limits of Justice.* Cambridge: Cambridge University Press.

Saunders, P. (1989) The meaning of 'home' in contemporary English culture. *Housing Studies*, 4(3), 177–92.

Saunders, P. and Williams, P. (1988) The constitution of the home: towards a research agenda. *Housing Studies*, 3(2), 81–93.

Savage, M., Allen, C., Atkinson, R., Burrows, R., Méndez, M. L., Watt, P., et al. (2010). Focus Article. *Housing, Theory & Society, 27*(2), 115–161.

Savage, M., Bagnall, G. and Longhurst, B. (2005) *Globalization and Belonging.* London: Sage.

Save the Castro. A kind of war, *Save the Castro Collection.* Can be found at: GLBT Historical Society, 657 Mission St, Suite 300, San Francisco, CA 94105.

Scheepers, P., Gijsberts, M. and Hello, E. (2002) Religiosity and prejudice against ethnic minorities in Europe. *Review of Religious Research*, 43(3), 242–65.

Scheff, T. J. (2006) A theory of runaway nationalism: 'love' of country/ hatred of others. www.soc.ucsb.edu/faculty/scheff/, accessed 11 December 2008.

Scheffer, P. (2007) *The Country of Arrival [Het land van aankomst].* Amsterdam: De Bezige Bij.

Schinkel, W. (2008) *The Moralization of Citizenship in Dutch Integration Discourse.* Amsterdam: Amsterdam Law Forum.

Schinkel, W. (2010) The virtualization of citizenship. *Critical Sociology*, 36(2), 265–83.

Schor, J. (1991) *The Overworked American: The Unexpected Decline of Leisure*. New York: Basic.

Scientific Council for Government Policy [Wetenschappelijke Raad voor het Regeringsbeleid] (2007) *Identification with the Netherlands [Identificatie met Nederland]*. Amsterdam: Amsterdam University Press.

SCP (1998) *25 Years of Social and Cultural Changes [25 Jaar sociale en culturele veranderingen]*. Rijswijk: Sociaal en Cultureel Planbureau.

SCP (2006) *Emancipation Monitor 2006: Changes in Living Conditions and Life Courses [Emancipatiemonitor 2006: Veranderingen in de leefsituatie en levensloop]*. The Hague: Sociaal en Cultureel Planbureau.

SCP (2010) *Emancipation Monitor 2010 [Emancipatiemonitor 2010]*. The Hague: Sociaal en Cultureel Planbureau.

Seligman, A. I. (2005) *Block by Block: Neighborhoods and Public Policy on Chicago's West Side*. Chicago and London: University of Chicago Press.

Seward, R. R., Yeatts, D. E. and Zottarelli, L. K. (2002) Parental leave and father involvement in child care: Sweden and the United States. *Journal of Comparative Family Studies*, 33(3), 387–99.

Simmel, G. (1984) Female culture. In G. Oakes (ed.), *Georg Simmel: On Women, Sexuality, and Love*. New Haven: Yale University Press.

Sleegers, F. (2008) The Limits of Feeling at Home: On Home Feelings of Transnationals [Grenzen aan thuisgevoel: Over het thuisgevoel van transnationalen]. MA – thesis, University of Amsterdam.

Sniderman, P. M. and Hagendoorn, L. (2006) *When Ways of Life Collide: Multiculturalism and Its Discontents in the Netherlands*. Princeton: Princeton University Press.

Somerville, P. (1997) The social construction of home. *Journal of Architectural and Planning Research*, 14(3), 226–45.

Stein, A. (2001) *The Stranger Next Door: The Story of a Small Community's Battle over Sex, Faith, and Civil Rights*. Boston: Beacon Press.

Stryker, S. and van Buskirk, J. (1996) *Gay by the Bay: A History of Queer Culture in the San Francisco Bay Area*. San Francisco: Chronicle.

Szasz, T. S. (1961) *The Myth of Mental Illness. Foundations of a Theory of Personal Conflict*. New York: Hoeber-Harper.

Tandogan, Z. G. and Incirlioglu, E. O. (2004) Academics in motion: cultural encapsulation and feeling at home. *City and Society*, 16(1), 99–114.

Tate, L. (1991). San Francisco, California. In J. Preston (ed.), *Hometowns*. New York: Penguin, 273–6.

Thiranagama, S. (2007) Moving on? Generating homes in the future for displaced northern Muslims in Sri Lanka. In J. Carsten (ed.), *Ghosts of Memory*. Oxford: Blackwell.

Tonkens, E. (1999) *The Regime of Self-Development. The Pertinence of Dennendal and the 1960s [Het zelfontplooiingsregime. De actualiteit van Dennendal en de jaren zestig]*. Amsterdam: Bert Bakker.

Tonkens, E., Hurenkamp, M. and Duyvendak, J. W. (forthcoming). *The Inept Society*. Basingstoke: Palgrave Macmillan.

Tuan, Y. (1975) Place and experiential perspective. *Geographical Review*, 65(2), 151–65.

Tuan, Y. (1977) *Space and Place: The Perspective of Experience*. Minneapolis: University of Minneapolis Press.

Tuan, Y. (1980) Rootedness versus sense of place. *Landscape*, 24(1), 3–8.

Turner, J. and Stets, J. (2005) *The Sociology of Emotions*. Cambridge: Cambridge University Press.

US Census Bureau (2010) Current Population Survey. www.census.gov/cps/, accessed 30 September 2010.

US Department of Labor (2009) *Employment and Earnings*. Washington: Bureau of Labor Statistics.

Uitermark, J. (2010) Dynamics of Power in Dutch Integration Politics. PhD dissertation, University of Amsterdam.

Uitermark, J., Rossi, U. and van Houtum, H. (2005) Reinventing multiculturalism: urban citizenship and the negotiation of ethnic diversity in Amsterdam. *International Journal Urban and Regional Research*, 29(3), 622–40.

Uitterhoeve, W. (2000) The Netherlands and the others: European comparisons from the Netherlands Institute for Social Research [Nederland en de anderen: Europese vergelijkingen uit het Sociaal en Cultureel rapport]. Nijmegen: SUN.

Urry, J. (2000) *Sociology beyond Societies: Mobilities for the Twenty-first Century*. New York and London: Routledge.

Urry, J. (2010) Mobile sociology. *The British Journal of Sociology*, 61, 347–66.

van der Graaf, P. (2009) *Out of Place? Emotional Ties to the Neighbourhood in Urban Renewal in the Netherlands and the United Kingdom*. Amsterdam: Amsterdam University Press.

van der Veer, P. (2006) Pim Fortuyn, Theo van Gogh, and the Politics of Tolerance in the Netherlands. *Public Culture*, 18(1), 111–24.

van Reekum, R. (2010) As nation, people and public collide: Dutchness and the culturalization of citizenship. Paper presented at the American Sociological Association Annual Meeting, Atlanta, 13 August.

Verhaar, O. and Saharso, S. (2004) The weight of context: headscarves in Holland. *Ethical Theory and Moral Practice*, 7(2), 179–95.

Verkaaik, O. (2010) The cachet dilemma: ritual and agency in new Dutch nationalism. *American Ethnologist*, 37(1), 69–82.

VWS (1995) *Beyond the Common Path: Program for Intersectoral Policies for People with Handicaps 1995–1998 [De perken te buiten. Meerjarenprogramma intersectoraal gehandicaptenbeleid 1995–1998]*. Rijswijk: Ministry of Health, Welfare, and Sport [Ministerie van Volksgezondheid, Welzijn, en Sport].

Walters, W. (2004) Secure borders, safe haven, domopolitics. *Citizenship Studies*, 8, 237–60.

Walzer, M. (1983) *Spheres of Justice: A Defense of Pluralism and Equality*. New York: Basic.

Watt, P. (2009) Living in an oasis: middle-class disaffiliation and selective belonging in an English suburb. *Environment and Planning A*, 41, 2874–92.

Weintraub, J. A. and Kumar, K. (eds) (1997) *Public and Private in Thought and Practice: Perspectives on a Grand Dichotomy.* Chicago: University of Chicago Press.

Welshman, J. (2006) *Community Care in Perspective. Care, Control and Citizenship.* Basingstoke: Palgrave Macmillan.

White, E. (1980) *States of Desire: Travels in Gay America.* New York: E. P. Dutton.

Wiggin, R. (1991) *Save the Castro Collection.* San Francisco: Save the Castro.

Wikan, U. (2002) *Generous Betrayal: Politics of Culture in the New Europe.* Chicago: University of Chicago Press.

Yang, P. Q. and Rodriguez, E. (2009) The case for staying home: myth or reality? *International Sociology*, 24(4), 526–56.

Young, I. M. (2005) *On Female Body Experience: 'Throwing like a Girl' and Other Essays.* Oxford and New York: Oxford University Press.

Index

145